THE ROMAN STUDENTS; OR, ON THE WINGS OF THE MORNING

THE ROMAN STUDENTS; OR, ON THE WINGS OF THE MORNING

Deborah Alcock

General Books

www.General-Books.net

Publication Data:

Title: The Roman Students
Subtitle: Or, on the Wings of the Morning
Author: Deborah Alcock
Reprinted: 2010, General Books, Memphis, Tennessee, USA
Publisher: T. Fisher Unwin
Publication date: 1883

1

THE ROMAN STUDENTS; OR, ON THE WINGS OF THE MORNING

CHAPTER I.

THE DEATH-DAY OF AN EMPIRE.

was one of the supreme moments in the worlds history, the death-day of a great empire. The city of Constantino was in the hands of the Ottoman. Through long, slow ages had the glory of the Eastern Cagsars waned and paled, until the very name of Greek, with all its glorious traditions, had become almost a synonym for the mean and treacherous vices of unscrupulous weakness. Luxury, licentiousness, fraud, and discord had eaten out the heart of the Eastern Empire. Sadder yet, the light that was in her had become darkness. The Eastern

Church had stiffened into clay, slain by the frozen breath of formalism and superstition. The Scribes and Pharisees, who sat in the seat of Chrysostom the golden-mouthed, tithed mint and anise and cummin, they fought about the use of the razor or the composition of the consecrated wafer, while they omitted the weightier matters of the law, judgment, mercy, and truth. Proud of their jealous orthodoxy, they too often forgot to regard the Triune God, whose mysterious nature they were so careful to define, as the living object of faith and love. Proud of their resistance to the adoration of what they technically styled images, they were quite as guilty as their "Western brethren of worshipping idols which could neither see, nor hear, nor walk.

Thus the Church was ripe for the judgments of God; and the State–the old Byzantine Empire–was falling to pieces from its own corruption, before the deadly sweep of the Ottoman scimitar chased it Into the gulf of things that have passed away for ever. For there is no resurrection for dead empires. They are judged here and now.

Who shall say why a falling state or a falling cause so often robes itself for death in new dignity and glory? Gleams of moral grandeur shine forth, tempting us to think that, if shown a little earlier, they might have averted the doom, which they only come in time to make us weep over. Not of an individual alone has it been often true that–

"Nothing in bis life
Became him like the leaving of it."

If we look the stern Muse of History steadfastly in the face, we shall sometimes see, even in her saddest moments, a smile pass over it, as though she knew the end of the Lord, that He is pitiful and of tender mercy. Often has He turned away His wrath from the vanquished, in the midst of their calamities, and " spoken comfortably" to that very generation which has received from His hand double for all her sins, and the sins of progenitors tenfold more guilty. Many a monarch has found a more bitter, but none a more honourable death than the last Constantine and last Caesar of the Greeks. It is a noble figure that meets our view, kneeling in prayerful vigil on the tesselated pavement of St. Sophia, receiving the memorials of his Divine Masters love, asking pardon humbly of all whom he had wronged, and then going forth, resolved to die for his people and with them; as he did–for after the assault, the body of Constantine was found by the victorious foe " where the dead were lying thickest."

But the broad stream of a nations destiny is ever breaking into innumerable ripples of individual life. The day that saw the Empire of the Eastern Cassars overthrown, witnessed also the terror and agony of a whole population. Each unit in the crowded city had a tale of wrong and suffering, or of hair-breadth escape and joyful deliverance. The horrors of a great city taken by storm are utterly beyond our conception, and we have, happily, no help from experience–so we can but try to look through the eyes of a few of those who were themselves actors or sufferers.

Into a small obscure church in a poor quarter faithful slaves had borne their wounded master, and laid him down to die. Count Eaymond Chalcondyles, a knight, a "Eoman," and one of Constantines most devoted personal adherents, sought death by his masters side, until, already mortally wounded, he was forced by the stream of fugitives through the breach in the inner wall, just rescued from being trodden to death, and carried to the little church, which was comparatively a place of safety, because too poor to tempt conquerors who had all the wealth of Byzantium at their feet. It was filled with a crowd of terrified women and children, but the picture-covered screen usual in Greek churches separated these from the dying man, who lay near the altar, on a couch made of church vestments hastily piled together. The priest knelt beside him, repeating prayers and psalms, and occasionally giving him a little wine from a chalice. The last rites of his Church had been already performed.

The dying knight was restless; his head turned wearily from side to side, his eyes sought the opening in the screen. "No one comes," he murmured. "Not yet

Have I done wrong to send for them?"

"Calm yourself, niy lord," the priest entreated; " think of your own soul."

"The best that could be done–the surest hiding-place that could be found–this little church," the knight persisted. "But oh! my son–my son! " He writhed in worse than bodily anguish as he saw before him the dead face of his gallant son, and thought of the dangers, more terrible than death, which that sons wife and child were braving even now. His faithful and favourite servant, who was also his foster-brother, had undertaken, at his earnest request, the dangerous mission of bringing them, in the disguise of slaves and by a circuitous route, from their own stately dwelling to this obscure place of refuge. In all the crowded city no spot was so full of peril that day as the marble palace of a patrician.

There was a pause. The dying warrior prayed in silence that these dear ones might not, at least, be taken alive. The priest murmured a psalm.

"0 God, the heathen are come into thine inheritance; thy holy temple have they defiled; they have laid Jerusalem on heaps. The dead bodies of thy servants have they given to be meat unto the fowls of the heaven, the flesh of thy saints unto the beasts of the earth. Their blood have they shed like water round about Jerusalem; and there was none to bury them."

All at once the dim eyes of Chalcondyles brightened, and he half raised himself, exclaiming, "Thank God! they come, they come!"

As he fell back, an old man, leading a boy by the hand, passed through the opening of the screen. " Thy lady, Manuel?" he questioned, anxiously.

"Safe–God and the saints be praised! " said the slave. "But, my lord, she hath swooned. I have left her in the care of the women. Here is our little lord."

The boy, a noble, manly little fellow of nine or ten, would have shown a courage worthy of his, race had there been only danger to meet, but the presence of death, now seen for the first time, struck an awe into his spirit. He gazed around him. with an amazed, frightened look in his eyes, and clung to the servants robe.

"Baymond, come hither!" said his grandfather. And Raymond, hearing the voice he loved, subdued his awe so far as to obey immediately.

Spell-bound by the solemn change in the dear familiar face, he did not weep, but stood, pale and trembling, beside the couch. He was remarkably beautiful, his form and features cast in the classic mould of the perfect Greek, with the fair complexion,

1 Spell-bound, he stood beside the couch."

golden hair, and blue eyes prized the more for their rarity, and the grace of free, happy, healthy childhood in every look and movement. Evidently accustomed to obedience, a sign from the knight made him kneel down close beside him, and take the cup from the hand of the priest, who retired to a little distance.

"Thou art but a child," said the dying man, in a low voice; " yet I must speak to thee, and thou must hear me, as though thou wert a man. For thy father is dead, I am dying, and thy mother lies unconscious. And thou, Raymond Chalcondyles, art left the only one on earth to bear that honoured name. Thou understandest?"

"I do," sobbed the child; for at the words, "Thy father is dead," grief mastered awe, and he wept.

"Listen then. This good priest will hide you here–you and your mother–with his own wife and children, until you can be sent with safety to Galata, and put on board a Genoese or Venetian ship. Our faithful Manuel has sworn never to leave you; and should the Infidel–which God forbid–he Ttnoios what to do. Remember, tis but one stroke; it will not hurt you. But, God sending you safe to Venice, I have already, foreseeing this ruin, forwarded a sum-of money, with a few books and jewels, to my good friend, the banker Benedetto. The money and jewels will maintain you; keep the books if you can. Obey your mother in all things, and should you be in distress or perplexity, ask counsel of Benedetto, for he is a wise man, and you may trust him utterly."

As he seemed to pause for an answer, Raymond said, still weeping, "I will do all you say, dear grandfather."

"Be a scholar. Remember thou art a Greek, heir to all that Grecian men have thought and done in the olden days. Yet not all Greek Give me the wine."

Raymond obeyed.

"I grow faint; yet there is that which must bo said. Bend thine head close, Ray mond, and I charge thee, forget not a word. It is a secret handed down in our house from father to son, never trusted to any keeping save that of the heir of Chalcon-dyles. Thou knowest we have an ancestor, a Frank, a Crusader?"

"Yes," said Raymond promptly. Young as he was, he knew his pedigree very well, and was very proud of it. " Raymond de Guiscard, Lord of Vaudelon, espoused the daughter of the great Chalcondyles. Their

"Enough. Now listen:–That Raymond de Guiscard owned, and lost, a rich inherit ance."

"I know:–Vaudelon is a stately castle, with a noble estate–vineyards, oliveyards, cornfields–in fair Provence, the best land God has given the Franks."

"I said owned and lost–lost it in a war righteous as ours against the Infidel, disastrous too as ours. Our ancestor resisted the tyrannical claims of the schismatic Latin Pope, as we orthodox Catholics do to-day. But De Guiscards castle was taken, his father slain, and he himself, a stripling, escaped with difficulty. Still, his rights remained, and have passed to us, his descendants.–More wine, Kaymond."

Eaymond, as he gave it, pondered what he could say to console his grandfather. What was it that he would have him do? He made a bold guess. " Grandfather, when I am a man I will go to the King of the Franks, and ask him to do us right, and give back our inheritance."

"Nay, my son; they who have kept it for two hundred years may keep it for ever."

"Then I will go to the Lord of Vaudelon, throw down my glove, and offer to fight him for it."

"Hush! Listen now, and act hereafter when thou art a man. Closer–my words must be few. The last lord, forseeing his ruin, buried in his ladys rose-garden a treasure of inestimable value. I know nothing for certain, but I suppose it to be a casket of jewels, priceless in worth and peerless in lustre. Our ancestor used to call it the luck of Vaudelon, and to say that whoso had it had nothing left to wish for, that castle and lands were well lost for it, and little worth without it. His father showed him the spot, and he wrote out, for his children, a description exact enough to enable any one who seeks with care and diligence to find it, changed though the place may be. The fragment of parchment is here, in my reliquary, with a lock of the blessed St.

Annas hair. Take it, wear it always, and lose it only with thy life." He placed a small, curiously wrought gold casket in the childs hand.

"Thou canst not read it now, for it is in our ancestors native tongue, which he called the tongue of Oc. But when thou art a man,–learn, read, seek, win,–and God be with thee. Till then, tell no one."

"Save my mother. I have never kept secret from her yet. Say I may tell my mother!"

"Well, she is discreet and virtuous. But none else; not even Manuel. And now farewell. God bless thee! Be true to Him and to the Faith."

"Dear grandfather," said the boy earnestly, " we are going among the wicked Latin schismatics; must I touch the accursed thing? " He meant the azyme, the unleavened bread, or wafer, used by the Latins in the Eucharist. So early may the iron of fanaticism enter into the soul; or, rather, so easily does the plastic material of a childs mind receive impressions from those around.

"Do, as child, what thy mother bids thee; judge, as man, for thyself. Now kiss me, lip to lip. Thou art like thy father, and thy fathers mother. No, no more wine. Is Manuel there? My eyes grow dim."

Manuel was there, and drew near his lord. Soon another glided in, strangely disguised in the capote of a slave or peasant, but with the face of a high-born lady, beautiful, though wild and wan. It was not lawful for a woman to come within the screen, but in that moment of agony and confusion the law was disregarded. The priest approached also, a sacred picture in his hand, which he held to the lips of the dying knight.

There was a solemn pause. Without was tumultuous noise–the shouts of those who slew and plundered, the cries of those who sought for mercy. Neither reached the closing ear of the dying man. He trembled no more for the living, he mourned no more for the dead. All things grew pale and dim. Even the rites and ordinances of his Church, even the forms and ceremonies that shut his soul in and closed around it like a cloud, seemed to melt and vanish away. Did One draw near instead, whose Face turns darkness into light? Feebly, from failing lips, the murmur came–" Kyrie eleison! Eyrie eleison me." And with that prayer, Chalcondyles passed into the presence of the Lord of Mercy.

A few days later Raymond and his mother were conveyed safely on board a Venetian ship, and bade a long farewell to the Golden Horn and the smiling shores of the Bosphorus.

CHAPTEB II.

THE QUEEN OF THE ADRIATIC.

HE Queen of the Adriatic proved a kindly nurse to the little Greek exile. She gave him all that childhood needs–love, home, friends, beautiful surroundings for his life. Had the noble widow of Chalcondyles and her son come destitute amongst them, the merchant princes of Venice would no doubt have had compassion and opened their well-filled purses to succour them. But fortunately the only charity needed was that of sympathy and neighbourly kindness, and it was freely given. The wealthy banker to whose care they had been com mended (by birth a Jew, but by creed a Christian) fulfilled his trust honourably and wisely. The sum of money which had been placed to their account, and which was augmented by the sale of most of their jewels, he lent at a rate of interest which would awaken the despairing envy of a modern speculator. In Florence at that time money-lenders usually exacted tliirty-three and a half per cent. It is true that these enormous gains were weighted, according to the universal law of compensation, with two great evils, obloquy and insecurity; still it was possible for a banker of high character to obtain very handsome terms for his clients, together with honour and safety. Benedetto did more; he found them a suitable and commodious dwelling at a rent merely nominal. A marble palace in the Square of St. Mark, or on the Grand Canal, might have suited the rank and the former fortunes, but it would have accorded ill with the present circumstances of the Grecian lady, while a meaner lodging in the city would have appeared to her in the light of a bitter degradation. The difficulty was solved by Benedetto finding a friend willing to share with her a good though modest dwelling in the island of Murano, famous for painters and for workers in glass. Here she lived in dignified retirement, holding little intercourse save with her fellow exiles, but regarded by her neighbours with the respect due to her rank and her misfortunes. Besides the ever-faithful Manuel, who remained through all vicissitudes constantly attached to the family of his master, she had but one servant, a Venetian woman. She practised the most careful economy; delicious fruit was cheap and abundant, and formed the chief luxury of their simple board. Only one expense was never stinted: Kaymond went as bravely clad as any young patrician of his age, and attended the first academy of the city, amongst high-born youths, who only awaited their majority to inscribe each an honoured name upon the pages of the Golden Book.

. Thus four years passed away quietly and uneventfully. After such an interval we may find Eaymond again one summer afternoon–in that happy climate there is summer eight months out of the twelve–taking his homeward way, book in hand, through the narrow footpaths that thread the city, and render it possible for those who desire it to dispense with the aid of the gondola. It is a beautiful city upon which he looks, with his. young eager eyes. "A city of marble, nay, rather a golden city paved with emeralds; for, truly, every pinnacle and turret gleamed or glowed, overlaid with gold or bossed with jasper. Beneath, the unsullied sea drew in deep breathings to and fro its eddies of green wave. Deep-hearted, majestic, terrible as the sea, the men of Venice moved in sway of power and war; pure as her pillars of alabaster stood her mothers and maidens; from foot to brow all noble walked her knights; the low bronzed gleaming of sea-rusted armour shot angrily under their blood-red mantle folds. Fearless, faithful, patient, impenetrable, implacable–every word a fate–sate her senate. la hope and honour, lulled by flowing of wave around her isles of sacred sand, each with his name written and the cross graved at his side, lay her dead. A wonderful piece of the world. Eather, itself a world."

Of this wonderful world the boy of fourteen saw as little and as much as boys generally see of the world in which they grow up to manhood, and which influences them so deeply. He took the loveliness and the grandeur as a matter of course, as part of the daily bread on which he lived; yet he did not really enjoy them the less on account of this simplicity and unconsciousness. Nor was he out of harmony with his surroundings. The sorrows of his childhood had passed and left no trace, save a few remembrances rather sweet than sad. Perfect in form and feature, and with the clustering golden hair many a Venetian lady envied Buskins "Modeim Painters."

him, simply yet tastefully clad in a sky-blue tunic with silver clasps and buckles (for blue was then the fashionable colour, and Raymond, before all things, must be fashionable), he trod his pleasant path, singing low and half unconsciously a fragment of a Greek song.

Still there was a little cloud–a very little one–on Raymonds clear brow that day. Even in Venice one has something left to wish for. It was not that he was unsuccessful at school. Good abilities and the happy accident of owning Greek as his native tongue (even though it was but the barbarous Greek of the Lower Empire) enabled him to take a high place, and to give his masters signal satisfaction. By his companions too he was beloved; but with one exception, and this exception was " the little speck within the garnered fruit" that spoiled his enjoyment. The schoolfellow who happened to be the object of his profound and fervent admiration–and no hero-worship is more enthusiastic than that of the boy for the youth a few years his senior–was the only one who regarded him with indifference, if not with dislike. As he walked and sang he pondered, in an under-current of thought, what way he should take to win esteem, whether by brilliant disputation, by Latin verses, "pure Tully every line," or by Greek chorus rendered into musical Italian numbers–for in these things the studious youth of that generation placed their joy and pride.

Presently he paused. He was now about to turn into the Fondaco Nuovo, and he found himself standing close to one of the many palazzos whose marble steps reach down to the limpid emerald waters of the canal. A little fruit-seller–member of a class characteristic of Venice, whose children were merchants from the cradle–had stopped near the same spot, overcome with weariness. Sleep had surprised him, half-standing, half-reclining against the lowest pillar of the portico, one bare brown knee resting on the pediment, while the other sturdy little limb still partly supported his body. His modest stock in trade, consisting of a dish, a knife, and half an enormous melon, lay at his feet. Raymond stood and looked at him. " What a picture he would make," he thought; " or, still better, a little marble statue. Wait now,–if I had only a bit of clay."

His wish was granted to the letter, though not at all in the spirit. Just at that moment " a bit of clay," a morsel of the muddy ooze of the canal hardened into an effective pellet, struck him smartly on the forehead.

The transformation was instantaneous and complete. His eyes kindled, an angry flush mounted to his cheeks, the blue veins in his forehead swelled and tightened like cords. After a moments quick glance around him, he flung his book, a MS. worth its weight in gold, on the step beside the fruit-sellers dish, and sprang dauntlessly into the midst of a knot of young men who stood at the corner of the street.

There was a rivalry of long standing, half jest, half earnest, between the inhabitants of the two halves of Venice, called re-. spectively Nicoloti and Castellani. Though this was properly the affair of the gondoliers., or at least of the class from which they were drawn, the nobles, and even the Doge, condescended to take sides, partly for amusement, but more from motives of policy. The young gentlemen of the Aoa-demy were not likely to prove indifferent to what afforded continual opportunities for the display of personal prowess. They chose to consider themselves Castellani, like the Doge, preferring to band together under the standard of the district in which the Academy was situated. Eaymonds, assailants were a band of Nicoloti, through whose quarter he was passing, and who probably had some mischievous pranks to avenge on the young academicians. They were therefore more than a little angry, and perhaps a little unfair. It was one of the laws of those street combats that no weapons were to be usedj but this prudent rule was often disregarded, and Raymoud-received upon this occasion some severe blows from heavy staves. Mad with passion, he struck right and left, dealing vigorous but unscientific blows. But his assailants were too numerous, and the contest too unequal to last long. He felt blood trickling from his wounds, and then a sense of faintness and a feeling of utter despair stole over him–though still he had no thought of asking for quarter. He just managed to put his back against a wall, and to utter once more, in a languid but defiant tone, the war-cry of the Castellani, when a loud " Sciar! " in a voice he knew, changed everything.

A gondola put its prow to the land close beside him, and a young man leaped from it and came to his aid. One of the rowers followed, and the scale thus turned, the conflict ended in the utter discomfiture of the Nicoloti. Raymond, to his great joy, recognized in his deliverer the object of his boyish admiration, Theodore Benedetto, the Phoenix of the Academy, as he was styled on account of his brilliant abilities. He was a tall, slender youth of about eighteen, dark-haired, dark-eyed, with features that showed his Jewish extraction, and with much of the striking physical beauty that often distinguishes the youth of that nation.

"Step into my gondola," he said to Eaymond; "I will take you home."

"Murano is far out of your way," Eaymond objected.

"I have no way; I sail for my pleasure." Then with a quick glance at Eaymonds face, "What! going to play the girl? " he asked sharply. " Eest a moment here." He beckoned to the httle fruit-seller, who, awakened by the noise of the quarrel, had been looking on with great interest, and at the same time keeping guard over Eaymonds book. This Theodore took from his hand, and gave him a piece of money and a command.

But his sharp words and scornful tone roused Eaymond more effectually than wine. "No," he said, shaking off the momentary weakness; " it is nothing; I am quite well," and rejecting the proffered aid of Benedetto, who, even in rendering a service, had contrived to implant a sting, he stepped into the boat. Benedetto followed, bidding the rower await the return of their little messenger from the nearest wine-shop.

The gondola was a private one, luxuriously fitted up. A delicious sense of rest and ease stole over Raymond as he reclined on the soft silken cushions, while Theodore drew the crimson curtain close, making a rosy twilight in the little cabin. The wine having been brought, Theodore made him drink some of it; and then, as they glided softly and swiftly over the still waters of the lagoon, he began without ceremony to examine his hurts. " Do you not know I am to be a physician?" he said, when Baymond would have resisted. "Already I understand such a simple matter as this. And you will naturally wish to save your lady mother a little uneasiness."

Raymond felt the force of the last argument. Besides, he could not contend the point; his schoolfellow had him in his power. A little water from the crystal flask that lay on the table, a fine white kerchief from the looms of Cambray, and a pair of gentle, firm, skilful hands soon accomplished the task. Theodores words sometimes missed their aim, and hurt where they meant to heal, his fingers never. Their very form–long, slender, sensitive–evidenced at once fineness of perception and exquisite dexterity.

Meanwhile the schoolfellows talked of the unfair and dastardly conduct of the Nicoloti, and formed plans of revenge. What they said was commonplace enough, but they speedily established a friendly understanding with each other.

"I had not known you were destined to be a physician," said Raymond. " Is not that to sacrifice your genius and your learning?"

"I do not see it in that light; but if it were, my father wishes it."

Physicians were highly honoured in Venice. They took rank with the nobility, many of whose privileges, in matters of dress and etiquette, they were permitted to assume. Eaymond was not of an age to understand how attractive these advantages for his son might appear to the Jewish banker, who–however wealthy and respected–was still condemned to stand outside the jealous circle of Venetian nobles, with the sense of a definite and rigid line drawn between him and them. He knew indeed that Theodore Benedetto was the only student in the Academy whose fathers name was not in the Golden Book; but he only thought with pride of the signal abilities of his hero, which had procured him entrance there. He loved to repeat the words of the learned " Grecian," Francesco Filelfo, the light of Venice and the glory of the Academy, who had expressly stipulated that Benedetto was to be amongst his pupils, saying that his class-fellows " might be glad hereafter to have their names immortalized with his."

(But do you like it? " he asked simply.

"Passably. A physicians studies are like all the rest, I suppose–all words and names."

Raymond looked at him curiously.

"I have heard you say that before," he said. "When your themes are praised, or your verses, you look as if you care nothing, and sometimes you murmur, All words and names."

"Is it not so? " asked Theodore. " We spend our lives learning what old Greeks and R-omans said about the things they saw, instead of seeing things for ourselves. Where is the use?"

Raymond did not know what to say, and therefore wisely said nothing. Already he was steeped to the lips in that admiration for antiquity which was the ruling passion of his day; so that Theodores words, had he allowed himself to criticize them, would have seemed to him open heresy. But his respect for Theodores abilities and learning made him prefer to assume that he had mis understood him, or was not clever enough to comprehend his meaning. So he turned to a practical question.

"Do you intend to finish your studies at Padua? " he asked.

This was the general custom of young Venetians.

"No; at the end of this year I go to the school of medicine at Montpellier."

"And I," said Kaymond, with a little air of shyness, which showed that he was revealing a favourite and cherished dream–" I hope one day to go to Eome, and to complete my studies at the new Academy there."

"We are near Murano," Theodore said, drawing back the curtain. " Look!"

A scene of beauty burst upon their sight. It was the glorious sunset of Venice, dear to poet and to painter. "The sun was setting behind the Venetian hills; great violet clouds crossed the sky above Venice. The tower of St. Mark, the cupolas of St. Maria, and that forest of spires and minarets which, rises from all parts of the city, painted themselves in black on the sparkling shield of the horizon. The sky was shaded in marvellous gradation, from cherry-red to cobalt blue; and the water, calm and limpid like glass, received the exact reflection of this immense radiation. Underneath Venice it looked like a great mirror of molten copper. The city, a black shadow between the sky and the living waters, seemed to float in a sea of fire, and looked like the majestic dream of the poet of the Apocalypse, when he saw the New Jerusalem descend from heaven like a bride adorned for her bridegroom."

Both gazed in silence, speu-bound by the sight. At last Theodore said–half raising himself and leaning his cheek on his hand, to gaze intently across the water at the spires and domes of the stately Ocean Queen–" Think, Lord Kaymond, all that lies yonder–the glory, the splendour, the wealth past counting! Think of San Marco alone–from gold-encrusted roof and alabaster wall to pavement of priceless marble–all beauteous with the spoils of the East. Nay, east, west, north, and south have brought their glory into thee, fair Queen of the Adriatic! Stately are thy palaces, but fairer still and statelier thy hundred churches. Trophies of war are in thee, for thy soldiers are strong of heart and hand; trophies of peace yet more precious, for thy merchants are the honourable men of the earth, and science, genius, art, have all conspired to consecrate thee." Then his tones grew measured, earnest, musical, until at last they became hah0 a chant, as he went on: " Thou sealest up the sum, full of wisdom and perfect in beauty. Thou hast been in Eden, the garden of God; every precious stone was thy covering–the sardius, topaz, and the diamond, the beryl, the onyx, and the jasper, the sapphire, the emerald, and the carbuncle, and gold. Thou art the anointed cherub that covereth, and I have set thee so; thou-wust upon the holy mountain of God. Thou hast walked up and down in the midst of the stones of fire. Thou wast perfect in thy ways, from the day that thou wast created, till iniquity was found in thee. With thy wisdom and thine understanding thou hast gotten thee riches, and hast gotten gold and silver into thy treasures. By thy great wisdom and thy traffic hast thou increased thy riches, and thy heart is lifted up because of thy riches. By the multitude of thy merchandise they have filled the midst of thee with violence, and thou hast sinned; therefore I will cast thee as profane out of the mountain of God, and I will destroy thee, 0 covering cherub, from the midst of the stones of fire. Alas, alas! that is true of thee, fair Venice, Spouse of the Sea, Queen of the Adriatic."

Adapted from " Lettres dun Voyageur." George Sand.

"What is it all?" asked Raymond, wondering. " Is it poetry?"

"Yes, from an old poem, older than Eschylus, in the tongue of my forefathers.–Stall!"

This, to the gondolier, meant turn to the right. They did so, and then shot up the narrow water street that forms the quay of Murano. A few strong, dexterous strokes of the paddle the gondolier uses for an oar brought them to the steps of a one-storied, but fair and substantial dwelling, with a front of marble adorned with quaint carvings.

"Come in," said Raymond; " my mother would like to thank you."

"Not now. Good night, sir." And Theodore raised his small woollen cap with some ceremony to his schoolfellow, who, as he was too proud to forget, was greatly his superior in rank.

But Raymond, with a happy instinct, stretched out his hand, and said frankly and warmly, "Good night, my dear Theodore. I am very much obliged to you."

CHAPTER III.

MOTHER AND SON.

jjoU are late to-night, Raymond," said the Lady Erminia Chalcon-dyles, raising her head as Raymond entered. Had a quiet, prosperous life been her portion, she might still have looked young; as it was, her dark hair was streaked with grey and her features were worn and wasted. She had been a beautiful girl, and was now a matron of noble presence, grave and stately. Gifted with great courage and strong passions, as well as with intense affections, her heart and her will had survived the shipwreck that robbed her of home, of kindred, and of friends. As the mariner clings to the floating spar, his last hope, so she clung to the child that had been left to her. In his young life she lived again; for him she was still enterprising, sanguine, ambitious; and, if all the truth must be told, for him she could even be worldly and selfish, she could plot and manage, as well as dare and suffer.

"I have had a fray with some of the Nicoloti," said Eaymond; and he eagerly poured out the whole story, making little of the hurts he had received and much of the help rendered by his schoolfellow, with a glowing panegyric upon whom he wound up the tale.

The Grecian widow was not a modern fine lady, to shudder at hearing her boy had been exchanging blows, or to shrink from seeing a crimson stain or two upon his dainty linen. She wished him bold and brave, as apt at play of sword and buckler as at grammar and rhetoric. So she only said, when he had finished, "I hold the banker Benedetto in high esteem, and have much cause to be grateful to him. I am glad you like his son. Still, I think your friendship, your intimacy, might be placed rather higher with advantage. At your academy there are the Mocenigi, the Loredani, the two Foscari, grand-nephews of the Doge"

"Who hold the Loredani in mortal hatred," Kaymond interrupted, laughing. "A fine choice of friends you offer me, truly! But I have fully made up my mind upon that subject–no Loredani for me. I hold by the Doge and the Foscari, and I hate Loredano and all his set!"

"Gently, my son. We are guests in Venice, and guests should avert their eyes from the quarrels of their hosts, and be very courteously blind and deaf to such things as in no way concern them."

"Blindness and deafness, when they are not born with a man, but learned in the way of business, have their limits," said Eaymond sharply. " Giacopo Foscari has been treated with horrible cruelty and injustice, and I care not who, hears me say it. The wretches who could torture a son in his fathers presence on the barest, idlest suspicion, and then banish him from his country unconvicted and uncondemned, would be capable of any crime. In fact, mother," he continued, not very logically, "I am sure the low-born rascals who set upon me to-day were of the Loredanis clients and workpeople; most of them are Nicoloti–at least, they favour that faction."

"If that be so," the lady said gravely, "my son must already have been far more outspoken than becomes either his age or his fortunes. But here is supper; I think you have need of it."

That was true; and the mother, while she forebore questions and condolences, was careful to supply her weary boy with strengthening food and good wine. He did ample justice to the meal, but had scarcely finished when he started up, exclaiming–

"Mother, I have thought of something; a good, beautiful thing. Say I may do it?"

"I will not say you may not, if I can help it. What is it?"

"You know that book of my grandfathers in the vellum cover with the gold clasp, lettered Beta?–the book of medicine, translated from the Arabic? May I give it for a present to Theodore? He is to be a physician."

"Ah, boy, it is easy to know thou wert born a prince! Are we so rich that we can give away a book worth a bag of gold bezants as if it were a melon or a bunch of grapes?"

"But I love Theodore; I want to give him a real, costly gift."

The lady pondered. " After all, Raymond, I know not if I ought to forbid thee. But for the care and kindness of Theodores father we might both of us have starved. We owe him our daily bread, our comfortable dwelling here, and, what I think more of, the opportunity of educating thee. It may be well to show our gratitude by a gift to his son. I will get the book, and if you like you can take it to him to-morrow.". "No," said Raymond, " not to-morrow; it would be like paying him for taking me out of the hands of those scoundrels. I will wait until Ascension Day, when everybody gives gifts to celebrate the marriage of the Doge with the sea. But, mother, let me have the book in my own keeping until then."

She went to a massive carved oak chest at one end of the room, unlocked it with a key that hung from her girdle, and brought out the precious volume, wrapped in a covering of purple silk. Raymond drew off the cover and examined the book with interest. "It is written by Maimonides, the court physician of Saladin," he said.

"I know thy grandfather used to hold it in high esteem."

"Yes; he said the books were not to be sold if we could help it; but he would not have forbidden us to give one away to a valued friend."

This allusion of Raymonds to his grandfather gave Lady Erminia an opportunity of asking her son a question which was often in her thoughts. At the time he received it the child had faithfully repeated to his mother his grandfathers dying charge, but since then he had never once alluded to the subject. Erminia did not wish him to forget it; she wished the thought to remain in his mind ready to awake in due time, but dormant for the present, because at his age much discretion could not be expected. If he began to dream and brood over it he might be tempted to mention it in confidence to one or other of his intimates. Therefore she said lightly, and as if it were a matter of no importance, "Dost remember what thy grandfather told thee of the buried treasure at Vaudelon?"

"Surely, mother," the boy answered, flushing; "I never smell a rose I do not think of it!"

"And why, in the name of St. Sophia? " "Why not, since my ancestor buried it in his ladys rose garden? Mother, I dreamt of it on my voyage hither–such a beautiful dream! As I lay in the palander, sick, weary, and frightened, I dropped asleep, and lo! it was summer evening, and I was walking in a garden of roses. Lovely ladies, with fair smiling faces, and clad in silken sheen, walked there too. They had all roses in their hands; and one, a little one, no taller than myself, but with soft dark eyes, and hair like a ravens wing, promised to be my guide, and to drop her rose over the spot where the treasure lay. Then I woke."

"Thou didst say nothing of it to me!"

"No."

"Why not?"

"I cannot tell." Children seldom can tell why they keep things secret, but they have very strong instincts about the matter, for all that. " Mother, where is Manuel? " he asked restlessly, for the aching of his bruises, of which he scorned to complain, together with the excitement of his days adventure, made him irritable and perhaps a little feverish.

"I think I hear voices in the studio, so I suppose he is talking with Giacomo " (the artist with whom they shared the house).

"Say quarrelling, mother. They never talk but to quarrel. I will go and see."

And Eayniond, anticipating some amusement, ran to the studio.

It was a large disorderly room, bare of furniture, but crowded with implements and objects belonging to more arts than one. The modern principle of division of labour did not prevail at that time, and two or three different arts were usually wooed by the same votary. Architecture, painting, wood-carving, and sculpture were in closest alliance; in fact the last-named art had hardly yet a separate existence, it was rather–as indeed painting and carving were also in a measure–the handmaid of architecture, that eldest-born and stateliest of all, whose masterpieces still astonish and delight the world. It was to decorate the shrine or the palace that the painter contributed his frescoes and the statuary his bas-reliefs. Moreover, there was yet another art–and really a fine art–which had at this time its head-quarters in Murano.

Giacomo was a little of all things; carvers tools, pieces of wood, and lumps of clay for modelling strewed the floor; on the rickety table lay a bunch of lilies, with their leaves, which he was essaying to copy upon glass; while in the corner, carefully veiled by a faded crimson curtain, stood an unfinished painting, which was to be his chef dasuvre, and was already his joy and pride, sometimes also his despair. He was a grey-haired man, with a mild, thoughtful, dreamy face, and clad in a tunic of brown velvet, much frayed and worn, and stained with many a spot of paint and clay. Before him stood the Greek in his long mantle, talking rapidly and with much gesticulation.

"Away with your graven images, which are no better than idols of Mahoun, breaking the holy commandments of God and the apostolic canons," he cried with a sweep of his gaunt arm. " You could employ yourself much better, Signor Giacomo, and in a manner more pleasing to God, if you would make a handsome frame for a real saint, a veritable holy picture, like this, which has been blessed by the Patriarch of Constantinople himself; " and he pointed to a miserable daub which lay upon the table, in staring red and blue, with a tinsel aureole round the head of the stiff, ungraceful figure.

"That a real saint! " the Italian exclaimed; " with no more shape in his body than an ell-wand, and no more expression in his face than a dead brick wall! That St. Nicholas of Myra! And you say he–he–was a doughty champion of the orthodox faith, and gave the heretic Arius a box on the ear at the Council of Mcaea? If that is at all like him he could have had neither power in his arm, nor speculation in his eye, nor fire in his heart."

"At least he had the true faith in his soul, Signor Giacomo; and he would have laid down his life rather than deface the image of God by shaving off the beard his Maker gave him."

"And making himself look like a priest of St. Marks," said Raymond, who had entered unobserved, the door being open.

Manuel stopped in some confusion. To the grief and shame of his heart his beloved lady had apostatized from the orthodox faith, and had obliged her son (decidedly against his will) to be confirmed according to the rites of the Latin Church. Manuels loyalty to her sealed his lips in Raymonds presence, yet this silence seemed almost a treason to his faith. Pitying his embarrassme-nt, of which he fully understood the cause, Giacomo said, "Che, Che! I will make your saint a handsome frame, Manuel; and," he could not help adding maliciously, "I will put in each corner the sweetest little child-angel you ever saw–just ready to carry the holy man to heaven."

"You will do nothing of the kind, Signor Giacomo; my prayers are poor things enough as it is,, without making them worse by saying them before-graven images, accursed of God and the holy orthodox. Church."

1 Well, my friend," the painter answered, " we will not quarrel; that, perchance, would do more to hinder both thy prayers and mine than a carved picture-frame. And how is my young lord to-night?"

"Well, thank you, Master Giacomo," said Eaymond, courteously. " Come to remind you of your promise to show me your picture."

Manuel, to whom the Italian style of painting was as abhorrent as was that of his own picture to the artist soul of Giacomo, suddenly remembered that he had pressing business. " I must go," he said, "and attend to my ladys accounts. By care and diligence I contrive that she shall not pay for anything more than twice its value, otherwise your Venetians, who are born for buying and selling, and nothing else in the world, would soon leave the fullest purse as empty as you left the shrine of St. Mark, at Alexandria, when you stole the saints body and hid it in a basket of pork."

This parting shaft did not tell upon Griacomo, who said quietly, "I was not born in Venice." When Manuel was gone, he continued, half to Eaymond and half to himself, "I was not born in Venice, but Venice suits me. I should like to know in what other city of Christendom could yonder honest fellow have his bearded priest and his leavened wafer to his liking; and the Jew his synagogue; and the Armenian his dark little closet of a church? God save the Council of Ten, say I! They do not like meddlers and busybodies, and they make criticizing the government a very dangerous game.–True, but then they mind their own business, and secure all other honest folk freedom to mind theirs."

Raymond, meanwhile, was investigating the contents of the studio, to which he was a frequent and privileged visitor. " May I have this lump of clay, Master Giacomo?

" he asked. " I saw to-day such a pretty little fruit-seller fast asleep on the step of a palazzo. I should like to try his figure."

"You are welcome to the clay, signor. But I hope you will use it better than the last, of which you made me a horse all legs and no body."

"How should I know? One never sees a horse here; I was but trying if I could recollect what the creature looks like."

"Go and study the horses of St. Mark! Boy, those divine creatures are from the hands of our fathers, who were greater than we–There were giants in the earth in those days."

"From the hands of my fathers, master painter," said the young Greek, with a glow of pride. " Can I look at those horses without sorrow–a proud sorrow, indeed–when I think how they were torn from my native city by the ruthless Crusaders? We are alike exiles and strangers, they and I.–But your picture, Master Giacomo, your picture!"

"You shall see it as it is, my young lord. But it is not finished–not yet." He sighed, then paused for a moment, almost reverently, before he withdrew the faded curtain.

A great poet has observed that it is the artists impulse to find expression for his deepest and dearest thought, not in his own art, but in some other. When his soul is moved to the uttermost, the poet would fain paint a picture, the painter write a poem. Probably this is because experience has already taught him the insufficiency of the form of utterance he can best use, and he vainly dreams that another might answer his need more adequately. It has been said that Giacomo was a man of many arts. It was his daily work to fashion elaborate friezes or delicate wood:carvings for the stately church which was then rising to be the glory of Murano. But he was also connected with both the things which made the little island famous, its school of painting and its glass works. On the one hand, he was the intimate friend of the celebrated Gentili brothers, whose genius rendered the school illustrious; on the other, he often painted dainty and delicate designs on the pure white lattimo, a rare glass resembling porcelain, which was one of the specialities of the place. Yet neither to marble, nor to wood, nor to precious tinted crystal would he trust what he tried to tell the canvas upon which Kaymond now stood gazing.

The picture was fully sketched, and partly painted. It had much of the richness, depth, and purity of colouring said to be the grand characteristic of the Venetian school, then in its infancy. The arrangement was stiff, and the grouping of the figures conventional; but the bright hues of the dresses–the sky–the grass–the trees–were put in with a loving appre-ciativeness, and graduated with an exquisite skill, which showed that, for the artist, the mystic chords of colour vibrated with thrilling harmony, and yielded, in and for themselves, that joy with which a stranger cannot intermeddle.

Kaymond saw how beautiful it was, and gazed on it for some time with real delight. " But what does it mean? " he asked at last. In the background were houses, indicating a city or town. A company of men–in number about a dozen–seemed to be coming from it into the country, which was merely a green place with trees. Three or four were depicted with much care, and near the spectator; Raymond knew by the dress of one of them, and the symbols he carried, that he was intended for St. Mark, the patron of Venice, though his introduction there was an anachronism. Two figures formed the foreground; one, fully finished, was pathetic in its air of helplessness and trust. It was that of a blind man, the sightless face–sad, wistful, full of pain and longing–turned hopefully to Him who was leading him. One hand was stretched out, as if from the habit of feeling his way, but the fingers, which were bent inwards, told that he checked himself in the act, knowing he might safely leave all to his guide. That guide held his other hand in his, and into those two clasped hands, the one holding, the other clinging, the painter had thrown all the expression of which he Was master. Not death itself, it seemed, could unloose that clasp. The figure of the guide was majestic, even the very folds of his robe had a calm and massy grandeur. But the face was only sketched.

"What does it mean? " Eaymond asked again.

"Do you not know? Our blessed Lord about to heal a blind man. The Gospel words are, He took him by the hand, and led him out of the city."

"Why have you left His face to the last, Giacomo? I would have begun with it."

"Because I cannot render it as I wish. Again and again I have tried, and failed." The old mans own face grew sorrowful. "It may be I am not worthy," he said in a lower voice, speaking to himself, not to Eaymond.

"Oh, nonsense! I know you can do it. Try again to-morrow. You have only to make a grand face, stern and majestic, such as will suit the Judge of quick and dead–an awful face."

Giacomo shook his head. " No, my young lord. You are wise and learned beyond your years, yet this is a matter of which you know not anything. The Face those opened eyes first looked upon was not stern, nor awful."

"Then what was it like?"

"I cannot tell. I cannot see it. Long and often have I sought for it. I sometimes fear " He stopped abruptly, remembering the youth of his listener, and turning away, began to busy himself in finding Raymond a suitable bit of clay. He gave him a few directions as to its use; but Raymonds energies were now beginning to flag, and his fatigue was making itself felt more sensibly. So he thanked the painter, bade him a laughing goodnight, and took his departure.

Left alone, Giacomo stood gazing sadly and wistfully on his unfinished picture. At last he murmured, "Shall I ever see that Face? Oh, that I knew where I might find Him! One look–only one–were worth dying for. Nay, I think I should die, broken-hearted with the joy of that one look. But I cannot see Him–I am blind. Jesus, Son of David, have mercy upon me! " Then after a pause, "But He took the blind man by the hand, and led him. That was before his eyes were opened. Has He my hand in His? Is He leading me? Then somehow, somewhere, sometime, I shall see His Face."

CHAPTER IV.

Theodores Family.

the opening year of the fifteenth century two Jews established a bank in the city of Venice. The enterpise was a bold and novel one, and it was crowned with signal success. The Jews enjoyed more peace and security in the island city than almost anywhere else during the Dark Ages. They that go down to the sea in ships, and behold the works of the Lord and His wonders in the deep, are not the stuff of which Dominies and Torquemadas are made. Fanaticism is a fungus that grows in vaults, secluded from the light and air of heaven; the winds thai fill the sails of merchant ships, the salt spray that dashes in the faces of hardy mariners are adverse to its life.

Because the Jews of Venice were more kindly treated than their brethren elsewhere, it followed as a natural consequence that they were less bigoted. It was rather with the indifference of curiosity than with shuddering horror that a son of the senior partner in the Jewish bank ventured one day into the cathedral, that he might admire the treasures gathered from the east, and west, and south to adorn the shrine of St. Mark.

It chanced that one of the great revival preachers of the Middle Ages, Fra Giacopo della Maria, then much celebrated for his eloquence and devotion, stood that day in the pulpit, and thundered mightily against the sins of Venice. Had he done no more, young Baruch might have gone away as he came; and the rather because his own life was so pure and sober that the fiery shafts of the preacher glanced aside from his armour of morality. But Fra Giacopo spoke of One who was wounded for our transgressions and bruised for our iniquities–of His sufferings, His patience, the guilty madness of those who slew Him, the atoning efficacy of His death. A conviction sank into the heart of the Jew that this was indeed the Messiah foretold by the prophets of his nation. He struggled against it, tried to put it aside, yet day by day " it did not pass, but grew." At length he applied for farther instruction, and for baptism. Some parts of his new faith, especially the adoration paid to the Virgin, to saints, and to images, jarred upon his feelings, and he never came to like them cordially; but he saw no alternative between his own creed and the Catholicism of the day, and he preferred the latter.

After this his outward circumstances prospered greatly. His conversion gained him the favour of the Christian community, while the storm it raised against him in the Jewish quarter died away gradually, and the sooner because his heart and hand were ever open to his "poor brother." His Jewish name of Baruch was softed into Benedetto, and under this apella-tion he became eventually the head of a prosperous bank of his own. He had all the virtues of the ideal merchant; his " word was his bond," he was honest, frugal, enterprising, sagacious, and the wealth which he won wisely he expended most liberally. Was there a festa to be got up, a church to be repaired, a bridge to be built, or a family of orphans to be rescued from penury, his townsmen knew the capacious leathern purse that hung at Messer Benedettos girdle would be freely opened. Therefore all Venice rejoiced when he found a bride in a wealthy and respectable Christian family; and all Venice mourned with him, when, a few years afterwards, his young wife was taken from him by an early death, leaving two little motherless boys. Benedetto mourned his wife long and sincerely, and did not seek a second alliance. But after an interval of several years, it happened that a mercantile correspondent in Spain appealed to his well-known benevolence on behalf of the miserable survivors of one of those terrible bursts of local fanaticism from which the Jews so frequently suffered. A horrible tragedy, enacted only too often, had just been rehearsed once again in Segovia. The Jews, a small but wealthy community, had been accused of the murder of a Christian child. Then followed plunder, imprisonment, torture, wholesale judicial murder. The Seville merchant wrote to Benedetto that only two children had escaped, and that even these helpless orphans were not safe in the Spains.

"Send them to me," was the prompt reply, and Benedetto named a Venetian ship soon to leave Seville, in which they could make the voyage.

The term " children" admits of great latitude in its application; as Benedetto thought when he welcomed to his house a beautiful girl of seventeen, along with a sickly boy two or three years younger. His first idea was to give the young lady a dowry and to marry her suitably, but it seemed impossible to separate her from her brother, who was in much weakness and suffering, and to whom she ministered devotedly. Not seeing anything else to be done under the circumstances, he extended his hospitality to both; and eventually the sorrows of the young Jewess, combined with her rich Spanish beauty, cast a spell over him which he could not break. She became his second wife, and the mother of Eaymonds friend, Theodore.

Benedetto soon found that his youthful bride was no child " whose character was as wax to mould." Material that once might have been plastic had been hardened in the furnace of affliction. A fanatical hatred to the Goim might be pardoned in a girl who had seen her father and two brothers perish at the stake. This hatred and a love equally passionate for her own race and religion seemed to fill her whole heart, scarcely leaving room for any other sentiment. To Benedetto himself she was reverent, obedient, grateful; that was all. But her childs young soul was the vessel into which she hoped to pour her own fervid passions; and rather from this than from any softer reason she loved him intensely. She had a fair opportunity for this transfusion of herself; until near the close of his eleventh year the boy was her pupil and constant companion. Her husband had consented, though unwillingly, to bestow on him her fathers Jewish name of Jonathan, afterwards transformed, a common process in those days, into its Greek equivalent (or what was nearest to an equivalent) Theodore. She determined to make her son, before all things, a Jew, and in this she was undoubtedly successful.

But whatever his nationality, little Theodore was no common child. From his earliest years he learnt with extraordinary quickness, and yet this quickness was not his most remarkable characteristic. He evinced a passion for knowledge; but it was chiefly knowledge of a kind that seemed to his contemporaries useless or trifling. No one knew exactly what he wanted, or how to give it to him. When, for example, he questioned his mother about the heavenly bodies and their motions, she told him how the stars in their courses, fought against Sisera. When he asked his father, he told him the uses of the Pole star, and how it guided merchant ships through the waste of waters. When he asked his teachers, they told him what the ancient Greek poets said about the stars. No one gave him the information he really sought, and consequently all left him unsatisfied and discontented.

After his mothers death, he entreated his father to send him to travel, like the great Marco Polo, near whose house he used often to linger, and who was the only Venetian hero whose achievements he regarded with any enthusiasm. ". I want to see strange countries," said he, "strangebeasts and birds, and trees, and what grows in the fields.

Instead of embracing this stormy and adventurous life, he was condemned to the students desk to be put in training for the role of a youthful prodigy, a kind of Admirable Crichton. The forcing system was then in vogue, and hot-house plants were at a high premium. The scholarship of the day was not wide, but it was exact and ardent. The classics, which were every ones passion, were pre-eminently attractive to youth; partly because the faculties which are usually strongest in youth, memory and fancy, were precisely those which they exercised, but still more because the youth was that of one particular generation, sharing, by a mysterious but well-known law, the impulses and inspirations of their sera.

Theodores abilities, which were universally acknowledged, were accordingly devoted to the study of Greek and Latin literature; and all Venice, which. had sympathized with Benedetto when it became too evident that his eldest son was growing up a spendthrift and a profligate, congratulated him that his youngest was proving the genius of the family; for by this time the bankers three sons were distinguished by lines too definite for a moments mistake. There was already the man of pleasure and the man of business, and now there was to be the man of genius. Benedetto himself was keen in his ambition for Theodore. Graetano, his first-born, had disappointed his hopes, though his career had been only too natural. In any age the son of a rich man readily becomes a man of pleasure; and the son of a rich man who is not noble readily becomes the associate of noblemen who are not rich, having wasted their substance with riotous living. The melancholy process by which a prodigal ruins his health, his character, and his estate, unhappily too easy in all great cities, was particularly easy in Venice. The noble city was fast losing the devout, sober, and frugal character that marked her earlier and brighter days, and beginning her rapid descent into what she has been ever since–the city of pleasure, of luxury, and of vice. She was now, as it seemed, at the culminating point of her glory and greatness, although under the surface the process of decay had already begun. " Iniquity was found in her."-

Antonio Benedettos devotion to the desk and the ledger equalled that of his brother Gaetano to the wine-cup and the gamingtable. From childhood Antonio had been a pattern boy, obedient, docile, assiduous. He had never given his father an hours serious uneasiness; yet it is to be doubted whether that father did not love the scapegrace Gaetano better than the steady Antonio, his partner and right-hand in the bank; for Benedetto felt keenly, though he shrank from acknowledging, even to himself, that this " his son that served him " was not quite of his own spirit and temper. His thoughts were less higb, his heart less large than his fathers. He was, if not too prudent, at least too calculating; he could open his hand liberally upon just occasion shown, but he could not, like his father, give " as a king," without reserve or afterthought; he was less the princely merchant and more the mere honest tradesman.

Thus Theodore became gradually the object of his fathers dearest hopes, as well as of the strong paternal love that has always characterized his race. He was not what is called an affectionate boy, but he was capable of strong attachments, and after his mothers death the only being he loved was his father. Partly to please him, partly to satisfy his own ambition, he became, with no real love for ancient literature, which indeed he rather despised, a distinguished classical scholar. The contempt he felt for his studies rebounded upon those who shared them with him. He contracted a habit of sneering at his own successes, as if they were things of little value, and it passed too easily into sneering at those over whom he obtained them. On this account, and not for his Jewish birth, which in latitudinarian Venice would readily have been condoned, he was unpopular with his equals. The silent flattery of Raymonds youthful admiration was all the more gratifying, and the accident of rendering him a service completed the attraction. When Raymond, with shy pleasure, presented the volume of " Maimonides," Theodore accepted it graciously, if without enthusiasm. He did not care much for the book, but he knew Raymond had few possessions except his princely birth; and his instincts were too fine to withhold from him the gratification for which he had made a real sacrifice–"the joy of doing kindnesses." And when afterwards the gift proved an unexpected treasure, as a sparkling stone given carelessly by a childs hand might prove to be a diamond worth a kings ransom, it seemed to Theodore, if not simply just, at least barely gracious, to acquaint Raymond with the fact.

CHAPTER V.

A TALK IN AN ARBOUR.

O, as I entered this place so will I leave it," said the aged Francesco Foscari to those who urged him to quit the stately palace of the Doges by a private way, and thus avoid the gazing crowds in the Place of St. Mark. For he was Doge of Venice no longer now; at length his enemies had won their wish and fulfilled their work. The torture and ban-ishment, and eventually the murder, of his innocent and only son, had not satiated the vengeance of Loredano for an injury which after all seems to have existed merely in his own imagination. The last drop in the cup of bitterness was the deposition of the aged Doge himself, after five-and-thirty years of patient and efficient service to as hard a master as any crowned tyrant–a jealous, cruel, and suspicious oligarchy.

The old man submitted, and veiled a broken heart under a proud and calm exterior.

"And leaning on his staff, he left the hall By the same stairs up which he came in state, Those where the giants stand, guarding the ascent, Monstrous, terrific. At the foot he stopped, And on his staff still leaning, turned and said, By mine own merits did I come. I go, Driven by the malice of mine enemies!"

The common people, by whom he was beloved, crowded the piazza to see him depart, and showed their sympathy by their reverently uncovered heads, their sighs and tears and murmured lamentations. But amongst those who stood nearest to the marble steps were Theodore Benedetto and Eaymond Chalcondyles; for their intimacy had progressed quickly, and they were now constant companions. Raymond had espoused the cause of the outraged Doge with a boys generous, reckless enthusiasm; and as the old man passed them by, his young clear voice rang out above the murmurs of the crowd, "God go with you, my lord! " Foscari heard, and his weary sorrowful face brightened for a moment. But others heard too. Theodore plucked his friend by the long falling sleeve of his overcoat. " Take care! " he whispered.

Not the present Giants Staircase, however–that was built in the sixteenth century.

"Ay, take care! " cried Raymond, " and let the foulest wrong ever done on Gods earth pass unreproved! Cowards, to hunt an old man down with such remorseless cruelty, and bring his gray hairs with sorrow to the grave!–But he heard me, Theodore; I could swear he heard me."

"I dare say," said Theodore drily; " you spoke loud enough. But let us get away from this crowd. Come to the Piazzetta. My gondola waits there."

They had a holiday; and Raymond was willing to accompany his friend wherever he wished to go. Theodore directed the gondolier to bring them to his fathers garden, a beautiful little islet laved by the soft waters of the lagoon, and blooming with rare and exquisite flowers. Here they left the gondola in charge of the rowers, and found themselves a luxurious resting-place, in a bower overgrown with roses and jessamine. There were many things Theodore wished to say, and he had chosen this quiet time and place on purpose. While Raymond sat, he preferred to recline face downwards on the ground, his hands supporting his chin. He began abruptly, "So you, who are not yet fifteen, think you have happened to witness the foulest wrong ever done in this world, which has lasted more than five thousand years? You talk of an old mans grey head. Did you ever see a boys grey head, Raymond? That is a sadder sight."

Raymond laughed incredulously. " Not I! " he said; " nor you, nor any one."

"Nay, but I have. Or at least, I have seen a man whose head was grey when his years were few as yours. It is not so very strange. There are many things which blanch the locks untimely. My father has a chart of the southern seas, sent to him by a friend in Lisbon, the work of a certain cunning draughtsman named Christopher Colon. His head has been white ever since he was thirty years of age. That was the work of thought and toil; but the young grey head I tell of was bleached by agony–bitter agony of mind and body. The boy was of our kindred, my mothers brother. Ay," he continued with intense earnestness, "we of Hebrew race are heirs to a heritage of woe that dwarfs the puny troubles of the Goim. Is there any sorrow like unto my sorrow? said our prophet-poet long ages since, and still the sad pre-eminence is ours. We are proud of it. We are kings of sorrow, crowned with anguish as with a diadem."

"But I do not think," Raymond interposed, " that is altogether true, here and now. Your father, for instance–he does not look very like an inheritor of woe." And Kaymond, as he thought of the genial, prosperous banker, could not help the sunny smile that rippled over his face at the incongruity of the idea.

"One here and there may escape the doom. I love my father well, but I hold by my mothers race, Kaymond. And this is how my uncles hair grew white at fifteen. He knew himself–that innocent-hearted boy–the murderer of father, mother, brothers–their blood was on his head."

"How could that possibly be?" asked Eaymond, now thoroughly roused and interested.

Theodore, before he answered, clutched a weed that grew near, pulled it up, and flung it from him with a gesture of bitter, angry contempt certainly not meant for the harmless green thing. Then he said, quietly enough–"Where they lived the Goim hated my people, because they were clever and industrious and therefore rich. So they invented a hideous lie–that the Jews, at one of their feasts, kidnapped and crucified a little Christian child."

"But who would believe such a story?"

"Those who would believe any absurdity under the sun–that is, those who choose to believe. Again and again, and in many different lands, has the same infamous falsehood, or that other, yet more monstrous, about poisoning the wells, been used as a weapon of destruction against us. We have even had companions in misery. I have heard that in France, long ago, thousands of unhappy lepers were tortured and slain under that last horrible delusion. Then, now, and ever the way of the world was, and is, to persecute those whom God has smitten."

"But surely, Theodore, the Jews and the lepers drank themselves of the same wells as their neighbours. Then why should they poison them? And what could they get by it?"

"Do you think men reasonable enough to ask and answer such questions as these would have let themselves be turned into the wild beasts that tore down the houses of the Jews in Segovia, and dragged their owners to prison? Not so. Given the fanatical fury of a few cruel bigoted shavelings, and the hypocritical greed of a few licentious spendthrifts who owed money they could not pay, and the rest was done by pure ignorance and stupidity. When I think of the tremendous power of ignorance and stupidity, how they rule mankind with a rod of iron, I am tempted to believe the world, like King Saul of old, given over by the curse of its Maker to those two spirits of evil, that they may possess and torment it."

"Yes, of course we scholars can afford to despise the multitude. They are ignorant and foolish," said Eaymond, complacently.

"Are we better, as scholars? Do you think playing at Greek, at Latin–do you think Homers verse or Tullys prose will renew the face of the earth? Would an oration of Demosthenes have given the rabble of Segovia the hearts of men, instead of the brute instincts of wild beasts?"

"I wish you would not talk that way, Theodore. No one. else does. Did you ever hear any of the Professors or Masters say such things? It looks so strange for the best scholar of us all, to talk as if he despised learning.–But go on, tell me of your mothers brother. How could all that have made him–that dreadful thing you said?"

"Cannot you guess? The Jews were accused and imprisoned without evidence. But there are means to make the accused their own accusers and the betrayers of their friends."

"The Question? " said Eaymond in an awe-struck whisper.

"Yes; what Giacopo Foscari suffered, and worse. Few have the strength of mind and body which enabled the Doges son to endure and be silent; and how could it be expected from a hapless boy–almost a child? What things he was made to say no one ever quite knew. He himself could only remember them afterwards as a patient remembers the ravings of delirium, which in truth they were. Enough. My grandfather and the other accused suffered the doom of fire. Only my mother and that unhappy boy were allowed to live, in cruel kindness. Compassionate friends sent them to my father, who gave them a home and afterwards espoused my mother."

"Do you remember your uncle?"

"Well. He lingered year after year, in a kind of living death, until I was about five years old. I used to amuse him, and he was fond of me. To little children all things alike are wonderful; I was accustomed to his grey hair and sad face, and never thought about them till my mother told me his story after his death."

"Theodore, we ought indeed to be Mends. We are both strangers and exiles, and have both horrible wrongs to remember, and perhaps to avenge."

"I am your friend, Raymond," said Theodore, and the words, from him, meant much. " But do not, I pray you, talk of your lot and your wrongs with mine. You have friends and kindred; to you, indeed, all the world is akin. Your home is everywhere. You think the same thoughts, you worship the same God as those around you."

"I own," Eaymond said candidly, " that I have never felt quite happy about the unleavened wafer. But my mother wished me to conform to the Latin ritual."

"Unleavened wafer! Latin ritual! " Theodore repeated with ineffable scorn. " Have you any conception how infinitely little these things look to a man who thinks the wafer only a morsel of dough, and Him they believe it is changed into only a " He caught himself up suddenly, bit his lip, and threw a quick glance around him. Not that he had really much to fear, even had his rash words been overheard, which was most unlikely. What has been called the Inquisition of Venice was purely an engine of State, far more likely to take cognizance of an expression of sympathy for the deposed Doge than of disbelief in the dominant religion. Moreover, indifference was the fashion; most of the great scholars of the age were not religious, and most of the great Churchmen of the age were scholars. Mitred abbots and courtly cardinals might have said as much over their wine as Theodore Benedetto had just breathed or hinted. But then they would have said it carelessly, and smiling, " twixt lip and wine-cup," keeping all the earnestness they possessed for the quantities of their Latin verse or the decorating of their palace walls. Theodore was right in thinking that such scholarship would never regenerate the world; but he was right also in his instinctive feeling that his own earnestness had better not be betrayed too plainly, since it showed his spirit the very opposite of theirs, one in which there was force and fire for good or evil, and therefore danger. At all events there was no use in shocking his friend.

But Raymond was not shocked. His own religious sentiments were well-nigh reduced to a few superstitions brought with him from the home of his childhood, and these were every day growing fewer and fainter. His plastic mind was bending unconsciously, but strongly, in the direction of the dilettanti semi-Paganism, which was then the scholars favourite religion. He looked at Theodore with just a little surprise, and said coolly–

"Why, how vehement you are! But I see now how it is, that, with all your splendid abilities, you do not like the Church. It is a pity. You might be a cardinal, or a bishop, or a dean, with a dozen fat benefices. And now, instead, you will only be a physician. Though," he added, in consideration for the feelings of his friend, " that is a very good thing too. You will make quite a magnifico, with a gold-headed cane and diamond ring, and doctors ermine-lined robe."

Theodore replied by a gesture of contempt. " I hated that only a little less than the other, until I read your book, Raymond. I thank you for that book; it is a right noble one, and written too by one of my people. Even yet the light comes from the East " (a kind of subdued glow passed over his own face as he spoke). " Moses Maimonides, philosopher and physician, was a wise man. He saio and he thought. That is better than all the learning in the world; for everything that exists is worth seeing. Even this root in my hand, that I have just pulled up, may hold a secret far more precious than those Greek roots we study at school. That is, if we have eyes to see. Thanks to you and Maimonides, I feel now as if I dare to use mine, and to think of what they tell me; nay more, as if it were in an especial manner the physicians business to do it. I have taken a long time and a devious way to thank you for your gift, Eaymond; but I do thank you. I wished you to know this–and me," he added in a lower voice. Then, with a change of tone, "Now let us explore the garden, and find, if we can, some roses worthy the acceptance of your lady-mother."

When they reclined once more in the luxurious ease of the gondola, Theodore said abruptly, after a silence of some minutes–" Do not misunderstand my words, Kay-mond. I am not devout. I shall never be a priest. But I fear God–the God of my fathers, the God of Abraham, Isaac, and Jacob–Jehovah." The last word was uttered solemnly, and after a reverent pause. Kaymond did not answer. In fact, he had nothing to say. The subject scarcely interested him, except so far that he wished his friend to believe and to do everything that was right, and nothing that was singular. His own faith was a dead one. He had no conception at all of God as a living Person, with whom he had to do.

CHAPTER VI.

AN EXILE.

LVE days afterwards the great bells that hung in the campanile of San Marco rang out their deafening peal over the hundred isles of Venice. The fair city had once more a sovereign. A new Doge, Pascale Malipieri, had been duly elected in the room of the deposed and outraged Foscari.

So Venice made holiday, as she loved to do upon every lawful occasion. The wealth of her sea-washed palaces had generated luxury, and luxury, in its turn, was generating idleness and extravagance.

The water-streets were gay with gondolas, richly ornamented and draped with the brightest of colours; the footways were thronged with citizens, whose stalwart forms and handsome bronzed faces were well shown off by holiday costumes of blue, white, and scarlet. But the crowd was densest in the Piazza–that glorious square, " beautiful for situation," over which San Marco, with his stately campanile, keeps majestic watch throughout the centuries. Beneath its shadow walked the merchant-princes, taking theirpleasure in their grave, decorousfashion, and discussing–it must be added with some reserve–the event of the day. Cloaks of silk or velvet, blue, violet, or scarlet (though the colour of their own cloudless sky predominated), lent variety to the scene. Nor were their ladies absent. Suitably attended, they moved amongst the gay throng, looking taller than their husbands–for the preposterous fashion of high pattens resembling stilts was then beginning to prevail–and attired in silken robes profusely adorned with gold and jewellery.

Some of the young academicians mingled with the crowd. They were dressed quite splendidly enough, though they had not yet assumed the long cloak that answered to the Roman toga virilis. As was usual now, the bankers son and the young Greek noble were found together. To Theodore, who had never made a friend before, the sense of companionship was delightful from its freshness, and the flood of Raymonds innocent hero-worship was still at full springtide.

"Look," said Theodore, as a pigeon fluttered over their heads and sought its resting-place in the eaves of the cathedral. " The pigeons of San Marco are the only inhabitants of Venice unmoved by the event of to-day. They at least live in peace, and are not the fools to set up a ruler one day and pull him down the next."

"I like to watch them," said Raymond, who had followed the graceful motions of the bird with brightening eyes. "I always bring a cake for them when I go to San Marco."

"What use? The State feeds them."

"What use? Just to see them eat. But look, Theodore; look at that lady–the tall one yonder, in the violet robe. How beautiful! what a face! what hair! The gold on her girdle is pale beside it."

One of their schoolfellows, a young noble, overheard the words, and laid his hand on Raymonds shoulder, repeating in a mocking tone, " What a face! what hair! Is that all you know, my innocent little Grecian? That is the wife of Signor Marco Tiepoli, of the Council of Ten; and I have seen the fair lady, every day for a month, sitting in her balcony, in a broad-brimmed hat without a crown, drying that dyed hair of hers in the sunshine."

Raymond laughed. " Like you, Francesco Buri. You can never let a man admire anything in peace. Theodore, what are you staring at?"

"That little girl–young lady. I think she is frightened by the crowd."

In Venice young, or at least unmarried ladies, were not wont to show themselves in public. They seldom went abroad, except to attend mass, and then they were closely veiled and carefully guarded. So the very presence in the crowded Piazza of a solitary young girl, still almost a child, and though simply dressed, evidently a lady, was a thing to occasion surprise and comment. The girls slight figure was enveloped in a fazzuolo, or long and ample gauze veil, beneath which she wore a plain brown dress. She stopped and looked around her hurriedly, as if undecided what to do next; evidently she was losing her presence of mind. It seemed as though she wished to cross the square; once or twice indeed she made faint attempts to do so, but abandoned them quickly, feeling the undertaking too formidable. Theodore saw that the rosy lips beneath the veil were beginning to quiver, and that a mist of coming tears was stealing over the soft dark eyes.

He stepped to her side. " Can we be of service to you, signorina? " he asked, in tones all the more reassuring because they were quiet and commonplace, and his manner was free from the fulsome gallantry then so usual.

"Oh, signor," said the child–for she was little more–"what shall I do? I cannot get home; and my grandfather is so ill."

"Whither do you want to go?"

"To San Lazzaro. We lodge beside the church."

"I will take you there, signorina. Allow me to carry this for you," and he took from her trembling hand the flask of rare wine which she had just purchased in one of the celebrated shops on the piazza. As she surrendered it she dropped a purse, very small and very light. Raymond, who of course had followed his friend, picked it up and handed it to her. " Best take a gondola," said Theodore to him. " Can you get one?"

Raymond shook his head. " We must walk," he said. "Come; I know the nearest way."

The guard formed–Theodore on the young ladys right hand and Eaymond on her left. At first few words were exchanged, and perhaps, had Theodore been there alone, the silence might have lasted the whole way. But Kaymond had no idea of foregoing the pleasure of hearing what such pretty lips could say. He drew from her that they were strangers in Venice, and that her grandfather was an exile.

"From Florence, I suppose? " he hazarded rather imprudently; and he took the answering murmur–whatever it was–for an assent, though the more keenly observant Theodore thought otherwise.

She was very anxious, she admitted; her grandfather was ill and unhappy, feeling hardly safe, even here; and an old servant was her only other friend and protector. " He was very sick to-day," she said. "Nothing does him so much good as this wine of Cyprus. Toinetta was busy and could not go out, so I went for it. I did not know the town would be so full."

This set both the cavaliers thinking. Raymond thought that he too was an exile–that the young lady was very beautiful–that he would get his mother to visit her. Theodore thought that they must be very poor, that Cyprus wine was costly, and that if it came anonymously from time to time as a present to her grandfather, she need never know who sent it. But, on this account, the more reserved he was now the better. So he held his peace, and yet, somewhat inconsistently, felt annoyed at Raymonds volubility. For the Greek boy and the Florentine girl (as she was supposed to be) harmonized quickly, and exchanged innocent confidences in the soft, musical, liquid tones of the tongue of Italy–not the Italian in which Florentine fishwives scolded and Venetian gondoliers swore and quarrelled, but such Italian as Petrarch whispered to Laura by the fountain of Vaucluse. When the narrow footways would not allow three to walk abreast, it was always Theodore who dropped behind.

At length they reached the gloomy building indicated by the young girl as her place of abode. It looked dark and forbidding, the doors and windows being closely shut and barred. But she rang a bell, and an unseen hand quickly opened the street-door. The wide staircase, common to all the house, was bare and dirty, and two or three rough-looking men, of the sailor or gondolier class, were standing in the hall, talking in loud, coarse tones, perhaps quarrelling. It did not seem well to our young cavaliers to abandon their charge until they brought her to the private door of her grandfathers "house," or suite of rooms. Here an old woman answered her low knock. "Holy Madonna! " she cried when she opened the door; " is it you at last? A fine fright you have given us! My poor master"

The girl interrupted her with a hurried inquiry for her grandfathers health.

It was always Theodore who dropped behind."

"He slept until half an hour ago, then he awoke and asked for you. Hush! there he calls again."

"I am coming, dear grandfather, I am here," said the young girl, with a heightened colour. She was hastening in, but recollected herself in time to turn and say to her two protectors, with the first touch of shyness she had shown as yet, "Signori, I thank you very much for taking care of me."

It was Eaymond, the younger of the two, who had the quickness to answer, "May we ask you in return, signorina, to make us your debtors by permitting us to kiss your hand?" A request the little lady graciously granted; but as she was evidently in haste to go to her grandfather, no more words passed between them.

As they retraced their steps down the gloomy staircase, Eaymond, who walked first, saw some bright object glittering on the ground. He picked it up, and it proved to be the broken half of a bracelet of silver filigree–a slight thing and of little value–which he had noticed on the wrist of their new acquaintance. He made no remark, but hid it, well pleased, inside his doublet. Theodore saw what he did, and smiled; but Raymond never saw that Theodore himself had already secured the corresponding half.

It was not until they had emerged from the narrow streets near San Lazzaro into the quarter of the city called the Rialto that either of them spoke. Then Raymond suddenly exclaimed–

"Theodore, I have seen her before!"

"Where? In a church?"

"No; in a dream. Walking in a beautiful garden with a rose in her hand."

Theodore laughed. His smile was very pleasant; but his laugh had a mocking ring that was not agreeable. However it was rarely heard.

"Wise men dream as well as fools," he said. "But they are fools who tell their dreams."

"Was Joseph a fool?" Raymond might have asked, but the story unfortunately was not familiar to him. He was far better versed in the legends of Greece and Rome than in the contents of the Sacred Scriptures. He said however, "That dream must have come to me through the gate of ivory."

"Well, if it did, I suppose you are awake now, and able to see that the crowds have doubled since the morning. How excited the people look! See that fellow standing up in the gondola, and haranguing the group on the traghetto, who are almost pushing each other down in their eagerness to press forward and hear him. Let us come too, and hear what he has got to say."

But at that moment Francesco Buri hailed them from another gondola, and invited them on board.

Receiving a gesture of assent and thanks, he bade his rowers put in for them; and scarcely had they seated themselves in the cabin when he said–

"Have you heard the news? The Doge is dead."

"What? The Doge elect?"

"The Foscari. There is one sad heart the less in Venice to-night, that is all."

It was true. The great bell of San Marco, which was rung to announce the appointment of a new Doge, tolled at the same time the knell of the deposed Foscari. He heard it as he knelt in prayer before the crucifix, and at the sound his grief-worn heart gave way at last. Thus the wicked ceased from troubling, and the weary was at rest. The aged passed away from a world in which the days of his pilgrimage had indeed been evil, at the same moment that the strong man was rejoicing in the fruition of his most ambitious hopes, and the young were dreaming, half unconsciously, their first bright dream of golden hours to come.

Well for Foscari if the angel of death found him, in very truth, beneath the Cross –not alone with bended knee before a graven crucifix, but with broken heart lifted up to One who was able to heal and save, because for him–and for us too–He Himself had gone down to the depths of agony, and tasted all the bitterness of human sorrow, pain, and wrong.

CHAPTER VII.
AVVENTURINE.

JOON after these things a little cloud began to arise in the serene firmament of Lady Erminias home life. Hitherto no son had ever given a widowed mother less uneasiness than Raymond had given his. But now a change was coming over him. It may have been the restlessness of his age. The boy was passing into the youth, fresh impulses were stirring his blood, setting "the old cheap joys " of childhood " in the scorned dust; " and with a new sense of strength there came a feverish desire to use it. He began to be irritable, sometimes even a little over bearing, in his intercourse with his mother, and fitful and quarrelsome amongst his young associates at the academy; though as yet such moods were but occasional, and his naturally sweet temper and genial disposition frequently asserted themselves, and won the victory.

Theodores influence saved him from some outbreaks; though it is doubtful, whether it was good for him to be the confidant of a young man so greatly his senior, and in ability the acknowledged phoenix of the school. But his most pressing danger arose from the indulgence of a quite natural and generous impulse.

The death of the aged Doge had created such excitement in Venice, and awakened so strong a feeling of indignation against the ruling faction, that the Council of Ten found it advisable to forbid all discussion of the affair Foscari " on pain of death." Yet Raymond, secure in his boyish frankness and fearlessness of consequences, persisted in discussing it, in season and out of season, at school and at home. He could not pass one of the Loridani, or their partizans, without a taunting allusion to it. He brought it even into his themes and exer-citations, a weakness of which a Grecian of that day, bound to care much more for the age of Pericles than for his own, ought to have been ashamed.

This was neither prudent nor safe under the rule of the jealous Venetian Oligarchy. The State Inquisition had often taken note of smaller matters. Moreover, the Venetian institution of the hired bravo was beginning even then to be useful to the unscrupulous, and terrible to the timid.

"You think," Raymonds mother remonstrated anxiously, "that because of your years you can say what you please with impunity. Do not flatter yourself. When the tongue is old enough to make mischief, the Ten may think the head old enough to answer for it. And even though the Signory might scorn your impertinences, the Loridani will not."

Of course she never seriously believed that the government would proceed to extremities against so youthful an offender; but she took up a strong position in order the more effectually to frighten her son, a manoeuvre which succeeded in this case no better than it usually does.

One day Kaymond came rather late into the lecture hall of the academy, where an assembly of boys and young men were sitting in respectful silence under the infliction of a dissertation on the Greek particles–most things being taught by lectures in days when books were scarce and costly. He seated himself as usual beside Benedetto, and taking out his tablets as if to make notes of the lesson, wrote down, "I have seen her again."

–" In a dream," muttered Theodore, and encouraged no more communications until the school had dispersed.

Then Eaymond told him eagerly, "I have found out who she is at last;–she is of the first quality. Her name is Viola. Frati is the surname by which her grandfather is known here, but it is only assumed to hide one far more illustrious. A Roman name, Theodore, not a Florentine, as I fancied. It is whispered that, in fact, she is no other than the orphan child of"

Theodore, without ceremony, placed his hand on his friends lips. " Are you mad? " he said angrily; " will you risk driving that brave man, and that helpless girl, forth from their last refuge–sick and almost dying as he is–and flinging him, as a victim, into the jaws of the Pope? Destroy his incognito, and you make it impossible for the Ten to connive any longer at his stay here, as they are doing now, from motives of humanity, and perhaps too from a little jealousy of his Holiness."

"I meant no harm," said Raymond, abashed. " Only I thought you would like to know who she is."

"Thank you!" said Theodore, briefly; and being a youth of uncommon reticence, he did not add, as he might have done, "I knew it all, and more, long ago."

When Raymond came home that evening, his mother received him with a smile on her lips, but with eyes heavy and red with weeping. She told him nothing until he had partaken of his frugal evening meal, which he dispatched quickly and in silence, aware from her manner that something of importance had transpired during his absence.

Then she said abruptly, for she had no heart for delay or concealment, "Raymond, you are to go to Rome immediately."

"To Rome, mother? that is joyful news indeed," cried Raymond, almost springing from his seat. " But how? When was it settled? Who has arranged it all for us, and so quickly?"

"Messer Benedetto has been here to-day. I expected his clerk or messenger, for our moneys are due, and he has never let the quarter-day pass yet; but he came himself. When our business was finished, he inquired kindly for you, praised your abilities and your progress, asked if it were not your intention to go soon to Rome for the completion of your studies, and spoke of the new Popes signal partiality for noble Greek youths, and great kindness to them. I said you were still very young. He answered significantly, that you were a man in understanding, though a boy in years. I spoke of next year–and then, Raymond, the truth came out. He recommended that you should go at once, and offered, most obligingly, any advances of money that might be necessary or convenient, with letters of credit upon Rome, and introductions that might be useful to you. I thanked him, but objected to hasty arrangements; and, in fact, showed that I was at a loss to understand the meaning of this in-sistance. And then he said plainly, that the air of Venice did not agree with you"

This was the formula, at once courteous and peremptory, by which the Inquisitors Pius II. (Eneas Silvius Piccolomini).

were wont privately to intimate to a foreigner that his further residence in the Eepublic was undesirable.

So after all they had condescended to notice Eaymonds boyish bravado! He was half flattered, half frightened at the perilous distinction.

His mother went on–" Benedetto wished to spare us as far as possible. Therefore he charged himself with the task of privately communicating the opinion of their Excellencies to me, merely assuring them that the hint should be duly given, and taken."

"Then we go next week–really next week?"

"You go."

Eaymonds wondering eyes sought his mothers face. Its expression of sorrowful determination explained the ominous word; and a torrent of inquiry, expostulation, entreaty, broke from his young eager lips. No one should part him from his mother. He would not listen to such a proposition, and he ought not. They should stay or go. together; she should come with him to Rome, or he would stay in Venice, and let the Council of Ten and the Inquisitors, do their worst.

"Be still and listen to me, my son," said the Lady Erminia, when the storm had spent itself a little. "Were I to go with thee to Rome, it would take all our slender resources, and more, to enable me to maintain a fitting position there, as thy noble fathers widow and thy mother. I must either beggar or disgrace thee. With the help of our Lady and the saints, I will do neither. But I can furnish thee forth–through the kindness of Benedetto, and the sale of the jewels that remain to us–after such a fashion that no blush need veil thy face amidst Orsinis and Colonnas at the court of the Pope. They say his Holiness is a patron of learning, and thou art learned for thy years. Use thy opportunities well; push thy fortunes; remember who thou art–the heir to noble memories and a noble name, but the child of a ruined house, who has to be the architect of his own fortunes.–What! weeping at thy age? I am ashamed of thee, child. Nay, I will not hear another word. Understand at once, that it is simply waste of breath to seek to change my determination. I love thee too well to listen to thee now. The thing is settled, and thou wilt thank me for it hereafter. I will pray for thee here, and do thou work for me and for thyself in Rome. Of course Manuel goes with thee. One servant at least is indispensable. Now fetch me thy gold and silver buckles, thy laces, and thy ribbons. I must see what there is to keep and what to buy."

Raymond, vanquished by his mothers strength of will, went into the next room to obey her, and to hide his tears–tears for which her shame was greatly misplaced. Had he quietly consented to her sacrifice, she might rather have blushed for him. But she had no relenting thoughts–no compassion for her own loneliness and desolation when the light of her eyes should be gone from her. She only pondered how, in the absence of Raymond and Manuel, she could live on a crust and a slice of watermelon, and send him the more, that he might go bravely amongst his young companions in the academy, and at the court of his Holiness. Pity that a course of action may be at the same time nobly unselfish and sadly mistaken!

An unexpected ally appeared, however, on Raymonds side of the controversy. The artist Giacomo knocked at the door requesting admittance. Having saluted the lady with great reverence, and at her invitation taken a seat, he explained the cause of his coming.

"Messer Benedetto," he said, "gave me a commission to-day to select from the glass works some rare and costly piece of crystal as a present to one of the cardinals whom he wishes to oblige. He said that your Excellency intended honouring his gift, and doubling its value by being its bearer."

"Yes, Master Giacomo, he spoke to me also on the subject. My son will bear it, and is glad to oblige Messer Benedetto. And you–is there any matter in which he could serve you in the capital of the world? I know him well enough to promise for him, if there be."

Giacomo made suitable acknowledgments. " Since you are so condescending, noble lady," he answered, "I will tell you of a matter that lies heavy on my heart, trusting to your discretion and to that of my young lord, your son. I must presume on your Excellencys goodness so far as to begin with a few personal details. My father was a Genoese, but my mother was a daughter of Venice, and a member of one of the families who guard jealously from generation to generation the secrets of our art–the art of working in glass and crystal. I had consequently the much-valued right of initiation, but I neither liked the work, nor prospered in it. It was far otherwise with my young brother, to whom I filled a fathers place, as we were early left orphans. He was soon known as the most promising apprentice of his time, and when he grew older he signalized himself by two or three inventions, adding brilliancy to the colours which are our pride and glory. But–I scarce know how–he awakened the jealousy of his fellow-craftsmen, and was at, length accused of what is, in their eyes, the most unpardonable of all sins–divulging the secrets of the craft. He fled, and, unhappily, without bidding me. farewell, or informing me of his destination. From that day to this have I never heard from him, or of him, and I know not whether he be living or dead. My fathers name was Salvi, but my mother was-a Morgagna, of a family well known here amongst the workers in glass. My brother may have adopted either name, or indeed any other that may have taken his fancy or suited his interest. Wherever he is–if he lives–he no doubt maintains himself by the art of which he is a master. It is just possible that the new Pope, who is said to be a prince of much taste, and a connoisseur in articles of vertu, and who is about to furnish a splendid residence for himself, might attract to his service a craftsman so skilled in a rare and difficult art. If therefore, your Excellency would make a few inquiries in Borne, you would lay your servant under the deepest obligation."

The Lady Erminia promised readily for her son, only stipulating that Giacomo should furnish him with the information necessary for identifying the wanderer.

This the painter promised gratefully, adding however, "Do not let my young lord give himself trouble, for while I would neglect no chance that offers, I think my brother more likely to be found in the South of France than in any part of Italy. I have lately heard of a company of glass-workers established there by the king in the mountains of Foix. Messer Benedetto, always kind and helpful, has promised to set inquiries on foot for me in that quarter. It only remains for me to ask what day your Excellency proposes to set out, that I may have the vase for his Eminence duly prepared and packed."

"My son and his servant propose leaving this next Wednesday, the feast of St. Per-petua."

"If your Excellency follows them later, and more leisurely, it seems better to me to intrust an article so fragile and costly to the care of your escort."

"I am not going at all, Giacomo."

"Indeed!" The painter looked surprised, but said no more.

"My son will do better without me, and for me the journey would be costly and laborious." The last word was a mere blind. She thought nothing of toil where Eaymonds interests were concerned; but she was reciting a lesson, saying first to Giacomo what she meant to say to every one on the subject.

Those who hold habitual converse with " things not seen" have sometimes an insight even into things seen which goes be yond worldly wisdom. They think clearly, and they tell what they think with calm and modest fearlessness. It appeared to the humble artist that the great lady before him was doing wrong, and he spared not to tell her so.

"Most noble lady," he said, with intense earnestness, " do you know what Rome is? The capital of the world it is true; but also the wickedest city in it. The residence of his Holiness; but the home also of spendthrifts, beggars, assassins. A city where the turbulent nobles are for ever flying at each others throats, and making their castles dens of rapine, licentiousness, and lawlessness."

"My good friend, you speak strongly. What of the Church? Does his Holiness, do their Eminences the Cardinals count for nothing?"

Giacomo mechanically looked about him for his tools: and not finding them seemed a little disconcerted. It would have been a great relief to his feelings at this stage of the discussion to saw vigorously through a piece of wood.

"I have nothing to say of the Church," he answered; " the world of course would be worse without it. I believe his Holiness, our new Pope, is a magnificent gentleman–learned, courteous, liberal. If Greek MSS.–if fair frescoes, and bas-reliefs–if pillars of marble and Corinthian capitals–could make sinful men pure, Rome might become the city of the saints once more. But they cannot. One may have all these, and prize them, and love to look on them,, and yet be no nearer God and Heaven. One may keep all the rules of grammar and rhetoric and break the Ten Commandments. Little comfort to you, lady, should your noble and gifted son grow to manhood a phosnix of learning and ability, a favourite of Popes and princes–and lose his soul hereafter."

The Grecian lady quailed somewhat before these bold words. Her conscience was not quite at rest. The question often arose within her, had she imperilled her childs soul by inducing him to join the Latin Church? So direly had formalism eaten into her heart that the sin of partaking of an unleavened wafer seemed far greater in her eyes than the sin of forgetting God, and living without reference to His will and word. Yet it was something that she believed in the loss of the soul as a terrible possibility; though she was not quite certain that it would outweigh the gain of the whole world, and was in midnight darkness as to how souls are lost–or saved.

She said, with a humility not very usual to her, "I know but little–I may make mistakes. Every one does sometimes. But I am doing the best I can for my son. After all, were I to remain by his side, there is litle in which I could change or influence him. The child must grow into the man. What manner of man God and the saints know, and they alone. Chance and fate must do the rest."

"Chance and fate, noble lady! " Giacomo repeated, with a mournful shake of the head. After a pause he added, "Your Excellencys words make me think of the Awenturine, which is one of the noblest triumphs of the glass-workers art."

"I never remember to have seen it." " It is rare and precious, because exceeding costly. Certain chemicals of great price and difficult to obtain are combined with marvellous care and skill, but I know neither what they are, nor how they are compounded, for those who understand the secret guard it as their lives. Yet all their art and all their pains cannot give them an assured result. Their treasure must be placed in a furnace hermetically sealed, and left there for hours unseen–untouched. Fate and chance must do their work in silence and in darkness. When the appointed hour has struck, the workman breaks the seal with a beating heart. It is an even chance whether he find a dull brown mass, fit only to be trodden under foot in a pavement of mosaic, or whether the glitter of ten thousand jewels shines upon his ravished sight, as the crowning glory of his art stands perfected before him. Something after this fashion, lady, as it seems to me, are you dealing with your noble and gifted son–your priceless treasure–sending him alone into the furnace of temptation, into that great city where the worlds fiery heart beats and burns ever more."

The-lady mused a space. Then she said, "I understand you. Be it so; I must take the chance. But you are a good man, Master G-iacomo. Pray for my son."

On the eve of Raymonds departure, Giacomo, with unwonted excitement and elation of manner, accosted Manuel, and entreated him to induce his lady and her son to honour the glass-works with a brief visit, that they might see the present intended for the cardinal, before it was packed with the care and skill that only professional hands could be trusted to bestow.

Manuel doubted they could spare the time, and rather made light of the matter, as he did, on principle, of all the arts and manufactures upon which the Latins prided themselves. But as the painter begged for so trifling a favour with an earnestness which to him seemed quite unaccountable, he promised to mention the subject to his mistress. Somewhat to his surprise, she consented at once, and Raymond was delighted to accompany her.

With deep respect of manner, but-without uttering a word, Giacomo escorted them to the room where the craftsmen were proudly exhibiting their masterpiece. The magnificent vase of crystal shone and glittered in the sunbeams, as if all the treasures of the mines of Golconda had been heaped together into one dazzling structure by some magic of the genii. Yet it was not its splendour so much as its artistic beauty that would have given it value in the trained eye of a connoisseur. The stem, the handles, the curiously wrought ornaments round the base and sides, seemed formed out of some rare precious stone, or rather out of some mixture of many jewels, fused into a mass of surpassing lustre and brilliancy.

"That is Avventurine," said Giacomo in a whisper to the Lady Erminia, while Ray-mond was frankly expressing his wonder and delight.

"Well has it prospered," returned the Grecian lady, while a smile, rare with her, kindled her sorrowful eyes and relaxed the lines of her anxious face.

"Noble lady, I take it for an augury," Giacomo answered, as his eyes turned from the glittering crystal to the graceful figure of the boy who was standing before it rapt in admiration. He did not add, as he might have done, that all the time the Avventurine was in the furnace, he had knelt in prayer for a successful issue.

"I, too, accept the augury," the Lady Erminia answered. " May such be the result of my Avventurine!"

"Amen, noble lady. Not chance or fate, but God, grant thee the desire of thy heart."

CHAPTER VIII.

THE ETERNAL CITY.

"Mother age, for mine I knew not,
Help me as when life began."

HOME in the Middle Ages–when the thought occurs, not to the professed historian and antiquarian, but to the general reader, a twofold idea floats before the mind. We think of the mighty dominant Church–that tremendous invisible power, ruling the souls and bodies of men with a rod of iron, sending heretics to the stake amidst the snows of Scotland, or missionaries to die on the burning sands of Africa–its hand everywhere, but its brain and heart, ever changing but ever the same, in that great city where the Caesars ruled and the martyrs bled.

Or, we think of the Eternal City herself, now a widow and desolate, torn and devoured by her own children, her hoary ruins trans-formed into the dens of robber chieftains–the Frangipani in the Coliseum, the Savelli in the Theatre of Marcellus, the Colonna in the Mausoleum of Augustus–lawless-ness, misrule, and violence everywhere, "blood touching blood"–the Kome for which Eienzi died in vain, because the nobles were too haughty, the plebeians too base, and all alike too selfish, to live aa brethren and freemen.

It was to this Eome that Eaymond Chal-condyles came in his frank, innocent, impressible boyhood. He brought letters of introduction to Cardinal Bessarion, his fellow countryman and fellow exile; and that eminent personage received him with kindness, and invited him to share the hospitality extended to several other young Greeks, who were aspiring under his patronage to the honours and emoluments of the Latin Church. Raymond, however, told the Cardinal at once, and with a candour somewhat unusual in the Greek of that day, that he had no thought of an ecclesiastical career.

"Most natural, my son," replied the suave and courteous prelate, who was equally a man of the Church and a man of the world. "You are the sole representative of a noble line, and it must be your care to continue it worthily. Still, remain with me. Go for your Humanities to your admirable Professor Pomponius Laetus, and for your pleasures to your equals, the young nobles of the great families here; and when you are old enough, I will undertake that you shall not lack employment suited to your tastes and your capacity."

Raymond acquiesced thankfully, and wrote rose-coloured letters to his mother describing his present enjoyments and his future prospects.

Rome ecclesiastical influenced him but slightly, if at all. He enjoyed the pompous ceremonial and the exquisite music of the Church; but he was not in any sense devout, and the prejudices of his childhood still hung about him, though of course he conformed outwardly to the Latin ritual. But there was a terrible risk that Rome temporal–the Rorne of his day and generation–would make him her own to his undoing. The dice-box, the wine-cup, the yet more insidious and intoxicating draught passion offers her votaries, were the deities worshipped by the young nobles with whom he associated.

The lust of the flesh, the lust of the eyes, and the pride of life ruled unchecked in their bosoms. They were, physically, a splendid race. Noble and beautiful to look upon was the young Italian patrician of the period, with gold-embroidered mantle flowing over his costly inlaid armour, his high-mettled steed obedient to his lightest touch, love-locks of ebony curling under his crested helmet, piercing coal-black eyes,-and bronzed cheek glowing with health–often too with passion; for his beauty was the beauty of the leopard or the panther, lending a lurid, transitory charm to a nature fierce, false, sensual, pitiless. Such were too many of Raymonds friends, and such–allowing for differences of race and temperament–might Raymond himself have become; but he was saved.

There was yet another Rome beside Rome ecclesiastical and Rome temporal. Another spirit dwelt in the Eternal City, haunting ruined temples, decaying arches, desecrated forums–a spirit strong with the strength of silence and of death, of love and reverence and memory, of all those unseen yet potent influences which mould the lives of men. It was the spirit of the past, the ghost of old dead Rome. In bygone days its shadowy hand had beckoned here and there some thoughtful student, who, raising dreamy eyes from his rare and precious parchment, obeyed and fol lowed the mysterious summons–like Cola di Rienzi, through strife and bloodshed to his own ruin,–or like Petrarch, through the gentler paths of classic song to the laurel wreath and the crowning on the Capitol. But now was come the hour when that spirit walked abroad through the length and breadth of the land; when that beckoning hand was seen, that spell of mysterious fascination felt, by all the eager, romantic, gifted youth of the day. It is almost always the young who adore the past; those for whom all the world is fresh and new invest the grey ruins of antiquity with the charm and the interest of the unknown.

Rome was then the head-quarters of a band of enthusiastic scholars with whom her language, her history, and her antiquities were a passion, and who very literally " delighted in her stones." To clothe her disembodied spirit once again with flesh, to bring back, in the fifteenth century, the days of Camillas and of Fabius, was the dream and the object of their lives. The Koman Academy, under illiberal or fanatical Popes a legal and theological seminary of the narrowest kind, had become in the days of Pius II. a noteworthy assemblage of literary men, who studied on the spot the monuments of a mighty ancient civilization, ancl not only spoke and wrote the purest Latinity, but sometimes even dressed and lived like old Romans.

The presiding genius of this school was Pomponius Laetus, a spare, uncouth little man, wrapped in a genuine Roman toga, who every morning, before daylight, took his lanthorn in hand, armed his feet with Eoman buskins, and trod the dark and miry paths that led from his modest dwelling on the Esquiline to the lecture hall on the Quirinal. There Raymond Chalcondyles and many another studious youth hung upon his lips, while with antique eloquence he praised those former days of the Eternal City, which indeed were better than these.

Eaymond had at first been attracted to the Eoman Academy and the teaching of Pomponius Laetus by the praises of a friend in Venice, who had formerly been his pupil; but he afterwards yielded to the fascination for its own sake, and, Greek though he was, became for the time as heartily absorbed in the Latin classics as if he had been born on the banks of the Tiber. Yet the spirit of the present world might eventually have proved too strong for the genius of the past, and pleasure have won him from his books, had it not been for an incident that occurred when he had resided for about two years in the household of Cardinal Bessarion.

One day, on coming home from the lecture hall, he met a Greek student, one of the cardinals proteges, who accosted him in some excitement. " Count Eaymond, your servant has been stabbed. I know he is a schismatic; but had we not better send for a confessor?"

"Send for a physician! " cried Raymond, who was deeply attached to the faithful retainer of his house. " "Where is he?"

Gregorio guided him to the hall where Manuel lay on a settle, the blood flowing freely from his wound. Raymond knelt beside him, staunched the blood with linen torn from his own dress, and lavished every tender care upon him, until the arrival of the Cardinals household physician.

It fortunately proved on examination that the wound was not very serious; and Manuel was soon able to give his young master an account of the transaction. He had been suffering from rheumatism, and one of the Cardinals pages good-naturedly recommended a visit to the miraculous Bambino of Ara Cosli, who, he said, had cured him of a broken arm with marvellous celerity. Manuel, very imprudently, called the Bambino " an idol," and denied its wonder-working power. The angry Roman replied that the leavened wafer of the Greeks was corrupt, and only fit to be cast to the dogs; to which Manuel retorted that no respectable dog would touch the accursed azyme of the Latins. The controversy had thus clearly reached the point where a stout hand might come to the aid of an angry tongue. The page was the first to strike, Manuel repaid the blow with interest, then the Italians stiletto flashed out and the quarrel ended in a crime.

Eaymond hotly espoused the cause of his servant, and sought the Cardinal, intent on procuring the condign punishment, or at least the dismissal, of the offending page. The Cardinal, bland, cool, and courteous as ever, requested an account of the transaction, which Eaymond had the rather uncommon honesty to give quite fairly, only softening the expressions used by Manuel about the host, a reticence that proved of no avail.

"No doubt, my son," said the prelate, himself a proselyte from the Greek Church, " the unhappy man used language yet more opprobrious in speaking of our holy mysteries, though very properly and out of becoming reverence you hesitate to repeat his words."

He then gave Eaymond clearly to under stand that such a scandal could not be suffered in the household of a Prince of the Church, and that, in fact, the question was not the dismissal of the page, but the instant dismissal of Manuel.

Raymond tried to remonstrate; but the Cardinal did not seem to understand the possibility of any one resisting his will for a moment. "Here, my child," he said, "take this purse of scudi, provide for the fellow handsomely, and trouble thy head no more about him. Be ready to come with me tomorrow to the Blessing of the Banners–nay, no more words now, I am busy. Good night, mio caro." And before he knew what he was doing Raymond found himself standing in the ante-room amidst a crowd of smirking pages, who guessed his business and rejoiced in his evident discomfiture and the triumph of their brother in office. Pride came to his rescue, enabling him to cover his momentary embarrassment. The purse was still in his hand; he had been obliged to take it from the Cardinal, or it would have

ec a fallen on the ground. " My friends," he said–there was a slight flush on his cheek, but he spoke in a tone of careless, good-natured superiority–" I am about to leave, for the present, the palace of his Eminence. You have all of you performed little services for me during my stay here; I therefore beg of you to divide among you a trifling largesse." And, flinging the purse on the table, he left the room.

His pride was sufficiently "philosophic and Roman" to be highly applauded by "the Master," as all the students called Pompo-nius Laetus, with whom moreover he was a special favourite. When, after telling his story, he intimated that he must now go and seek for lodgings, Messer Pomponio laid a rough but kind hand upon his shoulder, and said, in choicest Latin, "Let that be, my son; the little house on the Esquiline hath room for thee and me. It is true that olives and lentils, and perhaps a couple of eggs, with fresh water from the fountain, will be a poor exchange for the ortolans and beccaficos and choice red wine of his Eminences table, but at least they will be seasoned with liberty and with peace."

Baymond at this period thought Pom-ponius Laetus the greatest man in the whole world, an opinion shared by many of his fellow-pupils, whose envy he provoked by gratefully accepting the masters hospitality. Manuel also became an inmate of the house on the Esquiline, and, when recovered from his wound, worked diligently under the master himself in the celebrated garden on the Quirinal, where he cultivated with his own hand precisely the same fruits and vegetables as did the ancient Eomans, pleasing himself with the thought that he was following the example of Cincinnatus and Camillas–where too he often received his pupils and conversed with them under the shade of olives and evergreen oaks.

Baymond was now obliged, whatever his tastes might be, to embrace a life of severe simplicity and self-denial. Pomponius was determined to make this, his favourite pupil, a model of the genuine old Roman virtaes, dignity, moderation, self-control. It was, hard to expect the happy, free-hearted Greek boy to become a Stoic at seventeen; and as time passed on Raymond might have rebelled, had not exceptional circumstances reconciled him to his life of self-restraint. Already he had caught the true scholarly enthusiasm, and, under the fostering influence of Pomponius, it deepened day by day. That great master lived for his pupils, and wished to live in them for posterity, " like Socrates and Christ," as he himself said profanely;–a profanity very characteristic of his spirit and that of his school. They were the works into which he poured his ardent soul; for them, not for himself, he was ambitious. Like the poets perfect king, it might have been said of him–

"No keener hunter after glory lives,
He loves it in his knights more than himself,
They prove to Mm his work."

Under such auspices Raymond burned the midnight oil of the student, finding, for the present, joy and inspiration enough in " all the golden deeds of men," in the rich heritage of memory which the two noble languages, the Greek of his fathers and the cherished Latin of his admired instructor, opened out before him.

He, too, would be a " Humanist" and a great scholar; he would write commentaries and poems, edit classics, discover lost MSS., decide knotty points of antiquarian lore; he would become a power in the courts of princes, like Poggio Bracciolini and others of his type. Perhaps he would serve the learned and liberal Pope, whom he greatly admired for many reasons, but chiefly for his zeal in the cause of Christendom against the Turks.

Thus glided by very rapidly the tranquil days of a studious youth. Eaymond was likely to be the better, the braver, and the manlier all his life for the keen, cold, bracing air he breathed, and learned to love, during the momentous period in which character is formed and fixed. His manners, like those of Ms master and host, were severely simple, almost ascetic. Not that, in this particular, he was at all a type of the scholars of his age. No feature in the story of the Italian Renaissance is so sad as the divorce, only too general, between morality and learning. Bare indeed is it to find a great scholar who, like Vittorino de la Feltre, wore

"The white flower of a blameless life,
Amidst a thousand peering littlenesses."

When the literati of the fifteenth century quarrelled–and they quarrelled continually, and fought out their quarrels with weapons of all sorts; with epigrams, lampoons, epistles, and pamphlets, with fists, cudgels, and the daggers of hired bravos–wonderful and terrible were the. stories they told of each others doings and misdoings. With a large deduction for unscrupulous lying–in itself such a dark blot upon character–enough remains to show very clearly why that fair morning of intellectual promise never ripened into the full sunshine of a, glorious day.

Amongst so many gifted spirits, rich in noble capabilities, who were slaking their eager thirst at the unsealed fountains of ancient lore, we look in vain for one soul athirst for God, even for the living God. And "the people that forget God," however learned, intellectual, and refined, have usually contrived in all ages to end where He says they shall, and to make a hell for themselves with their own passions.

The Platonic mystic school, of which Pico della Mirandola is the type, stands exempt, at least partially, from this condemnation. Of him, and of those like him, we speak not here; they were but a small minority, and could not leaven the mass. The thought and culture of the day, especially south of the Alps, was essentially Pagan. Thus Eaymond Chalcondyles, under the very shadow of the Vatican, and a favourite with the Pope and with half the College of Cardinals, whose fashion it was to patronize rising young scholars, grew up a frank Pagan, with as little real belief in the God who made him as in the " Jove " and "Bacchus" whose names were continually on his lips. That he did not also, like the majority of his associates, grow up an open profligate he had to thank God–that God whom he had forgotten so utterly.

CHAPTER IX.

Raymond To His Mother.

Written in Modern Greek.

" Eoma.–Feast of S. Chrysogone.

feABEST OF MOTHEES,

"Joy and sorrow mingle in my breast as I take my pen to write to thee once more–joy that thou dost so long after me and desire to see my face, sorrow, that thou canst not come to me; nor can I go to thee, so far as seems to me at present. But I am about somewhat from which, if I succeed, I hope great things. You know the zeal of his Holiness against the Turks, whom all Christendom has cause to hate–though with hatred less desperate and deadly than yours. I have nearly completed an ode, delineating his Holiness in the character of Nestor animating the Greeks, after a partial defeat, to reunite their scattered forces and overwhelm the Trojans. It is written in Greek, but there must be a translation into the choicest Latin to please the Master, who–only think of it, mother!–has all his life refused the study of the tongue of Homer and Plato, lest it should spoil his Latinity. Should this affair prosper, and be favourably received in the proper quarter, I may find a purse of scudi wherewith to go and make holiday at Venice with thee, mother dear.

"I have, perhaps somewhat idly, undertaken another work of late, which has not furthered my studies. It is a secret, even from the Master; but I have no secrets from thee, mother. Thou rememberest of old how I used to beg bits of clay from good Messer Giacomo, and try to fashion them into the likeness of things that pleased me? Well–but I must tell my story from the beginning. Among our academicians are the two young Porcari, kinsmen of him who, under Pope Nicholas, came to so sad and terrible an end. The Master reverences the memory of Stefano Porcaro, and says he died a true Eoman, and for trying to restore the old Koman liberties, as did Eienzi a hundred years ago. And his Holiness is so humane and liberal a prince, that he punishes no man for words and opinions, be they never so bold. The Porcari have been allowed to return to the city and rebuild their palace, which they occupy unmolested. But Porcaros father-in-law, the most deeply implicated in his rebellion of any who escaped his doom, died in exile only a few months ago; and with him to the last was his granddaughter, Stefano Porcaros only child. Mother, dost thou not remember sweet Signorina Viola, whom I guarded to her home the day of the Doges inauguration? Thou sawest her, afterwards, at San Marco, and saidst to me, No fairer bud ever waited for the sunshine to unclose it. Those were thy words. If thou couldst but see her now, mother! Her kinsfolk have brought her hither, and though she lives in strictest seclusion, she attends mass every day at the church of Santa Maria Trastevere, where at last they buried her fathers outraged remains; and there she prays without ceasing for his soul. It weighs sore upon her heart that he died without shrift or sacrament. And indeed " (The words that followed here were carefully erased. Scholars, it is true, allowed themselves large liberties of tongue and pen; but even under a liberal Pope like Pius II. a reflection on the cruelty of one of his infallible predecessors, and one whose friend and minister he had been, was at least not seemly.) "I have seen many a Koman maid, with raven hair and laughing eye and coral lip, but Viola di Porcaros loveliness is of a different, and, as it seems to me, a far higher type. Our good Gia-comos art may do justice to the others, and his brush transfer to canvas their rich and vivid colouring; but that still, calm face, with its look of sorrow, purity, and peace–that slight girlish form, so full of grace and dignity, would need the chisel of a Phidias and a block of the whitest marble to do it justice. I have neither; still, though my better judgment disapproves, I cannot help spending my leisure upon a bit of clay, which is slowly taking features that might serve for those of the guardian angel of a good man who had fallen into mortal sin. They say she is to go into a convent;

but that would be a sore pity. However, I have written too much of this already; I must pass on to other matters. I pray thee to make known to our friend Giacomo that I have done all that in me lay to fulfil his commission, but have failed to discover any Salvi or Morgagna among the artists or cunning craftsmen of this city. And now I must tell thee what the Master said the other day in the lecture hall."

"What the Master said" would not possess the same interest for us that it did for Raymond, so it need not be given here. At this point the grey-haired, noble-featured woman whose wistful eyes had been devouring every word in the closely-written sheet, looked up and paused. " Poor boy–poor child! " she murmured. Then a large tear fell slowly, blistering the page. With an effort, and apparently without very close attention, she read what yet remained, then put the letter carefully aside and left the room.

She went to her almost empty jewel-case, to try if anything remained there precious enough to change for gold–gold that might defray the heavy expenses of a journey to Rome. But her search proved fruitless; everything of considerable value had been parted with long since.

She was right in the inference which she drew from Raymonds letter, though wrong in some of the conclusions to which it led her. a new element had entered the young mans life, an element like fire in glory and in strength, but also, like fire, terribje and dangerous. Henceforward the masters praise was no longer to be his dearest hope; neither was the love that watched his childhood to be any more his most precious treasure. So much the mothers boding heart understood too well.

What she did not understand was the "romantic" ingredient in her sons character, perhaps a legacy from his crusading ancestor. Eaymond Chalcondyles was no Eomeo, with passions rapid in their growth as Jonahs gourd, and fierce as the Eastern sun that smote it into death. He was rather a knight of mediaeval chivalry, enraptured with the sweet, far-off worship of his star, and well content to dwell for a while in the enchanted borderland of reverence, hope and aspiration.

CHAPTEB X.

OLD FRIENDS MEET AGAIN.

"Eoma, Eoma, Eoma,
Non e piii com era prima."

OPE PIUS, second of the name, slept with his predecessors–a motley crowd, whose shadowy forms haunt the imagination, some of them hideous as nightmares, like his whose horrible wickedness has doomed him, says the legend, to haunt the subterranean passages of the Eternal City restless until the day of judgment, "with the head of an ass and the feet of a bear; " others, less loathsome but more terrific, like Gregory VII., like Innocent III., who " caused their terror in the land of the living," and whose spectre hands still seem to grasp the keys with a regal air, as though vindicating their right to "lie in glory" amongst the kings and rulers of the earth.

Benedict VIII., who seems to have been as great a monster of wickedness as the more celebrated Alexander VI.

Eneas Sylvius Piccolomini was neither a Sixtus IV. nor a Julius II., yet he stands out in somewhat interesting individuality from the long and wearisome line of tiaraed shadows. We can afford to remember that he was a scholar and a gentleman; and, still higher praise, that he laid aside, in his old age, every meaner ambition in the endeavour to unite all Christendom against the common foe of all, the conquering Turk. Better far Pius II. than Alexander VI.; but better far than Pius II. any faithful servant, however humble and obscure, of that Divine Master whose earthly vicegerents wretches that would have disgraced the throne of the vilest Eastern despot blasphemously dared to call themselves.

No doubt Pius II. was sincerely mourned in Rome, and by few more sincerely tban by the Humanists of the Academy. Nor was it likely that the memory of his good deeds towards them would be " interred with his bones," when a successor of the type and temper of Paul II. had to be contrasted with him.

A selfish, narrow-minded bigot was now to occupy the Papal throne. It may seem incongruous to us moderns, who usually picture to ourselves the ecclesiastical tyrants of the Middle Ages as lean, cadaverous monks, worn with fasting and self-torture, that one of Pauls first acts was to increase the splendours and gaieties of the Eoman Carnival. But there was really no incongruity. The language of the bigot to the populace has often closely resembled that of the Epicurean to himself–" Eat and drink, for to-morrow you die–only be sure you leave me to take care of what happens to you afterwards." One stern prohibition always looms in the background of song and jest and festival, "Whatever you do, be sure you do not dare to think. That is the crime for which there is no pardon."

Eome has always been wise enough in her generation to recognize the danger of an open volume of St. Pauls Epistles; but not always have her pontiffs been sufficiently astute to discern the same peril lurking between the leaves of Homer, Virgil, and Plato. Bat if Paul II. really did so, he proved his penetration; for it was quite true that the fructifying germs of independent thought–so fatal to his system–were being wafted silently and secretly from soul to soul, from old dead Greeks and Eomans to young, living, passionate Italians, in whom the modern world was finding its beginning.

It was now the season of the Carnival. " The Master " had been absent for a considerable time in Venice, but his return was now shortly expected, and Eaymond hoped that his mother might be induced to come to Rome under his escort, and that of the friends sure to accompany him from the City of the Sea. Perhaps, however, the young Academicians enjoyed the festival all the more freely without him, since he would have insisted upon their taking their pleasure precisely as did the old Romans, or not at all. After a forenoon of fun and frolic, Raymond and some of his chosen intimates visited a cook-shop on the Corso. Divesting themselves for the time of masks and dominoes, they chatted gaily over their plates of brown and golden fritters, and their cups of red wine. It was soon decided that they should stay where they were and see the races; and Raymond and his chief friend, a young nobleman named Campano, discovered that both were to spend the evening at a banquet given by Cardinal Bessarion. The tolerant Greek had long ago forgiven Raymonds boyish petulance, and regarded him with kindly interest as a fellow-countryman and a promising scholar.

Not, however, ihejirst carnival after the accession of Panl II.; this was the carnival of 1408.

"-Call for me, my dearest Glaucus," said Campano, " and we will go gaily together."

Nearly all these young dreamers discarded their baptismal names, and called each other by fanciful classical appellations. Campanos was Callimachus Experiens, Raymonds was Glaucus.

"Gladly, my Callimachus. But, I pray you, let your servant attend us; for Manuel, though the best fellow in the world, is no philosopher, and when his blood is warmed with the Cardinals good wine, he is sure to favour the scullions and serving-men with some of his schismatical nonsense."

"I hear the incomparable Platina is not to be of our party."

–" Has another engagement. Hark–listen to that fool of a friar."

The young men paused in their talk, and listened to what was going on at another table.

A sturdy, bare-footed friar, robed in dirty grey, was leaning forward on his elbow in the eagerness of his conversation with a companion similarly clad. A dish heaped with savoury venison steaks was before them, and stronger wine than the temperate Academicians cared to drink sparkled in their cups.

"So I took the bones, having paid down the price," the friar was saying. " My heart misgave me as I counted out the good broad scudi; but I have turned the money over more than once since then–all for the good of our honourable house, of course. Thanks to all the holy saints, and especially to St. Cosmo, the second joint of whose little finger Che, che, my brother, what would you have? The good saint is popular. Every one does not go to sea, make journeys, gaze at the stars, but every one gets sick sometimes, or thinks he does. St. Cosmo sends in no doctors bills to poor men, heavy as St. Christophers burden, and long as"

"Long as a fools tongue. Hush! " said the other friar, with a warning glance directed towards a very different pair, who were seated at a third table, farther off from the Academicians. A gold-headed cane, and an ample and handsome robe, trimmed with costly fur, proclaimed one of these a physician, and a prosperous one. After the habit of physicians, he sat with head bent down " smelling his cane," its golden head being in fact a box filled with costly spices, reputed preventives against infection. Opposite to him, and full in view both of friars and scholars, sat a tall, grave-looking man, with grey hair, ample forehead, and eyes whose far-away expression contrasted strangely with the hard, firm lines of a well-cut mouth and chin. His garb, though decent, was that of the lower class; and Eaymond looked at him with interest–"A poor scholar, doubtless," he thought. But while he looked the face changed suddenly; the calm brow contracted, the pale cheek glowed, the lips unclosed and curled, and the dreamy expression passed from the eyes as they turned upon the friar a look of infinite scorn and indignation. Some caprice of memory recalled to Kay mond the amazement he felt one day at seeing Giacomo, the meekest of men, blaze out into sudden passion with a boy who was tormenting a dog. And thus he lost a good part of the friars story, to which his companions were listening with ill-suppressed merriment.

"What are you all laughing at, mio caro? " he asked his friend Campano.

"How they took him in at a rival house, drugged his wine well for him, and sent him off in the morning with a relic box filled with stones and rubbish, and no blessed bone of St. Cosmo to conjure with any more. Per Bacco! diamond cut diamond then, and no mistake. Just listen."

"Worst of all," the friar was saying, " at my next station, away there in the marshes beyond Velletri, there comes to me a grand lady, a marchesa, from the castle hard by. She leaves her page and serving-woman without, and asks to speak with me alone. Then she begins to weep–and never in my life could I bear a womans tears, were she but a contadina–not to speak of fair ladies here. Her only son lies shivering with the marsh fever, one touch of the blessed St. Cosmos finger would heal him, she was convinced of it, for she had had a dream about it; and she would give the Saint a double handful of gold pieces–her diamond ring–anything I chose to ask. Here was a strait for an unworthy son of St. Francis! Only to think of losing all that for our honourable house! Surely the blessed Saint himself inspired me. Signora, said I, after only so long a pause as you might say an Ave Maria in–signora, this matter is important; I too have had a dream about it. It is revealed to me that no good can be done until the Saint, whom your noble son hath hitherto neglected to honour, is propitiated by a night of fasting and prayer. Therefore go, my daughter, watch and pray; I too will do the same, and ere the sun has risen to-morrow I will stand at the bedside of the young man with the blessed Bone in my hand! She departed, content and hopeful. My brother," continued the friar impressively–" my brother, that night the Saint wrought a miracle. At daybreak, when I opened my reliquary, the bone was there. Behold it now!"

"Glory be to all the holy Saints! " the other friar ejaculated, while the Academicians stifled their laughter. One of them, whom his companions called Agathocles, whispered, pulling out a piece of gold, "Ill offer him this to tell me privately how he did it; whether he robbed the churchyard, or bribed some ass of a contadino to let him take up his patrons trade for once, and perform a surgical operation upon him."

Calm and clear above all rose the quiet voice of the grey-haired stranger. " He feedeth on ashes; a deceived heart hath turned him aside, that he cannot deliver his soul, nor say, Is there not a lie in my right hand?"

Every one turned to him at once with looks of amazement, but no one spoke. Indeed there was scarcely time. Half a minute afterwards the landlord ran in excitedly, "Signori, signori, you are losing the sport; the races are beginning."

The friars ran to the street, the knight of St. Cosmo hastily putting up his relics; but the physician and his companion kept their seats, apparently unmoved. Meanwhile the landlord beckoned the Academicians apart; they were excellent customers, worthy of especial favour. " Come to the balcony, signorini," he said.

They did so, and saw a gleam of gold, a blaze of scarlet, and a glitter of flashing weapons, as the Pontifical horsemen, splendidly equipped, galloped down the crowded Corso, clearing a way for the runners.

The runners–who were they? Of old the youth of Eome, fleet of foot and strong of sinew, would have held it fair sport to measure their prowess and activity; while from window and balcony the bright eyes of mothers, sisters, lovers, would have watched them and cheered them on. But oh, degenerate days! degenerate sons of sires who ruled the world! Now Eoman men and women, Eoman boys and maidens, thronged the Corso, shouting, yelling, laughing, jeering, every face alight with the fiendish joy of witnessing or inflicting agony. Yet, after all, were they so degenerate? With such eyes had their fathers gazed on the arena while gladiator stabbed gladiator to the heart, or lion from the Lybian desert tore unresisting Christians limb from limb. Along the narrow path, kept clear with difficulty, shambled and staggered a file of weary old men, whose grey hairs should have won them reverence, or at least compassion. Half clad, with ropes round their necks, a mark for the taunts and insults of the populace, who pelted them with mud and even with stones, they struggled on. No thought of a prize to be won animated their flagging powers; if any gleam of hope kindled those frightened, despairing faces, it was only the hope of reaching, somehow, the Church of San Marco, the goal of their race of agony;–and then being done with it all, and lying down to die. " Tis a shame! " said Agostino Campano, averting his handsome boyish face.

"The Holy Father does not think so; he thoroughly enjoys the sport," said some one else, pointing to a balcony almost opposite, decorated with costly tapestry upon which were wrought the arms of the Holy See. " I can see him laughing heartily."

"Ecco, what would you have?" asked the landlord. " They are Jews. It was his Holiness himself who thought of forcing them to run these races, along with the buffaloes and the asses, for the amusement of the Eoman people."

While they spoke one of the runners stumbled, fell, and lay on the Corso apparently dead. Perhaps it was the effect of the afternoon sun, or of the rich food and strong wine with which, in cruel kindness, these unfortunates were always plied; more probably it was the shame and ignominy that broke the old mans heart. There was a confusion of voices. " Let him alone! " cried some of the crowd. " Drag him away!" cried others, " he stops the path."

A fact. This disgraceful spectacle, begun by Paul II., lasted until abolished by Clement IX. in 1668.

Then those in the balcony saw the crowd divide, making swift way for one who passed through with an air of authority. It was the physician they had noticed below. Under the eyes of all Rome–Pope, cardinals, princes, ladies in the windows and balconies, people thronging the Corso–he advanced with rapid stride, and tenderly raising the poor old Jew, took him in his arms, covering him with his costly cloak.

There were cries and murmurs, which he did not seem to hear until one voice arose above the rest, "Let him be, Signor Doctor, he is only a Jew."

Then the physician raised a calm, pale face, and with a glance around him half contemptuous, half defiant, said distinctly, "He is my brother."

Eaymond smothered an exclamation of surprise, and turned quickly into the house.

"Are you going to help him? " asked Campano, stopping him. "If so, I am with you. There may be bloodshed. The Plebs is a surly beast, and likes to worry the Jewish dogs."

"That Jewish physician is my oldest friend," said Eaymond.

"Corpo di Bacco! this grows exciting. Come, all of you–old Eomans, Humanists, friends of liberty. Come and help our Glaucus!"

That however was not necessary. The populace only scoffed and growled a little, then all eyes were turned to the other runners, and the incident seemed forgotten.

In the meantime the scholar-like stranger had contrived to procure a litter, upon which the still insensible form of the poor Jew was laid, and the ragged bearers were induced by the promise of a large bribe to bring him to the Via Fiumara, in the quarter now called the Ghetto. The Jews were not yet con fined by the law within the narrow precincts of that miserable suburb, but it had been from time immemorial a dwelling of their race, though some Christians lived there, and many Jews inhabited the Trastevere, a district on the other bank of the Tiber.

"Whither away, Glaucus? " cried his friends, who during this interval had descended to the shop, as Eaymond, coming in from the street, slipped on his domino.

"I see my friend the doctor is going with his patient; so I must go too, if only to find out where he lodges."

"Wait a moment. We are making up a purse for your friends poor relation. Here, my Agathocles!"

The lads were freehanded; and Callima-chus, or Campano, who had set the collection on foot, soon gave Eaymond his own purse, heavy enough to place the poor old Jew above want for the rest of his life.

Little thought Eaymond, as he took the purse gaily, laughing his thanks, how that frank pleasant face would haunt his memory, that joyous voice ring in his ears his whole life long. He made his way after the litter down the crowded Corso, giving and taking many a good-humoured jest as he went, for it was the mad and merry time of the Carnival, and no man cared what he did in the streets of Kome.

"Theodore! Theodore!–Dr. Theodore Benedetto! " he cried breathless, placing his hand at last upon his friends shoulder.

The greetings that followed were all that could be expected between such friends after such a separation. Theodore had no difficulty in recognizing Kayinond, with whom the change from boy to man had been only a harmonious development. The Grecian palm had but grown after its kind from a graceful sapling into a stately tree. With Theodore the change was far greater; scarcely a trace of youth remained in the grave, melancholy face, the face of a man who had struggled and suffered, and perhaps despaired. After greetings came questions and answers, broken, disjointed, fragmentary, as such are wont to be when friends meet suddenly after a long absence.

Theodore had taken out his degree some years ago; that indeed Raymond knew already, as a few letters, though very rare and occasional, had passed between them; but he was prospering so well at Montpellier as a teacher of medicine and philosophy that his friends dissuaded him from returning to Venice. He had come to Rome upon this occasion solely " to visit his brethren."

"And who is " Raymond pointed, with a familiar Italian gesture, to Theodores companion, walking in front of the litter with a Jewish boy, a grandson of the sick man, who had appeared upon the scene mysteriously, and was now showing them the way to his house.

"My servant."

Raymond looked surprised. " He has the air of a scholar," he said.

"He is a scholar, and a good one. But he is poor, and he wished to come to Rome; so I offered to take him with me."

"A Jew?"

"A Christian–the best I have ever seen. Where do you live, Count Raymond?"

"Say thou, my Theodore, I pray thee." And thenceforth, as of old, the personal pronoun that marks intimacy was always used in their musical Italian.

Raymond gave the address of the Masters house on the Esquiline, which he still occupied, though the Master had long been absent, as his adopted son and the guardian of bis books and MSS. He mentioned with regret his Engagement that evening at the Cardinals banquet. " It would be disrespectful to absent myself," he said.

"True," returned Theodore, " scholars should not do these things."

Raymond laughed. " Not little scholars," he said; " great scholars like the Master may be as unmannerly as they please, and it makes them greater. But I need only show myself, and make my bow to his Eminence. I shall then slip away, and thou and I will have a royal night together. Come to me. I am now in sole charge of the Masters house, with Manuel, and a servant whom he left me, a stupid contadino. Bring your man; Manuel shall take good care of him.1

They had now passed by the stately ruins of the theatre of Marcellus, and entered the Piazza del Pianto–the "place of weeping," most appropriately so called. The little cortege was about to turn into a narrow filthy street, crowded to suffocation, and reeking with all sorts of offensive odours.

"Do not come farther," said Theodore sadly, for he was ashamed of the dwelling-places of his brethren. "I must now attend to my patient."

"As you will," Raymond answered. "Here is some medicine as likely to promote his cure as any you can prescribe," and he put the purse, with a brief explanation, into Theodores hand.

The shadow deepened on his face as he took it. " I have no doubt of my patients gratitude," he said. " At least here the Jew is learning well his lesson–to take the Christians insults with meekness, his favours with humble gratitude. Now farewell. We meet to-night."

CHAPTER XI.

OLD FRIENDS ARE PASTED.

T chanced that Eaymond through some misadventure failed to keep his appointment with his friend Campano, and went alone to the Cardinals palace. He stayed a short time, and then, according to his promise, returned home to await the visit of Theodore, who soon afterwards made his appearance.

Manuel had prepared for them an elegant though simple repast of fruit, wine, and confectionery. The tiny "atrium" where they sat resembled, as closely as antiquarian research could make it, the room where a Fabius or a Cincinnatus might have received his guests; the amphora that held the wine, the cups from which they drank it, the graceful lamp filled with olive oil in which a lighted wick was floating, were all strictly " after the antique," and wore the forms with which the remains of Pompeii have made us so familiar.

But the two young men who were wearing out the night in eager, passionate talk were not after the antique at all; their surroundings, contrasted with themselves, looked a pale and faded anachronism. They were not old Greeks or Bomans; they were men of the fifteenth century, men of the Renaissance, with the warm blood of a worlds new spring time flowing in their veins and its passions stirring their hearts.

Each had to hear and to applaud the others successes in the schools. Raymond told of his with modest and becoming satisfaction. His only serious disappointment had been the death of Pope Pius, which had not only deprived him, in common with others, of a kind patron, but rendered useless his ode upon the Crusade. Theodore spoke of his own achievements with something of the old cynicism; and yet even Theodore kindled into enthusiasm as he talked of his pupils, evidencing the joy every earnest thinker feels when he finds he can transfuse his thought into the souls of others. Eaymond, accustomed to see this passion strongly exemplified in him whom he reverently called " the Master," entered into it with sympathy and interest. " It must have been hard to leave such scholars," he said.

"Life is not all thought, it is action too," replied Theodore. " Needs must that I visit my brethren and look upon their burdens."

"Is the philosopher still so much the Jew?"

"Still? "Theodore repeated indignantly. " Know you not that for long ages the Jew has been the philosopher of the land of his exile? What hand but his has cherished and fed the lamp lit by the sages of the East, that else would have gone out long ago in the thick darkness of modern supersti-, tion? Who translated Averroes, annotated his immortal text, carried forward his sublime and daring speculations? While the Goim have been worshipping stocks and stones, and feeding the sluggish spark of intellect that remained to them on garbage like the tales of that friar we heard to-day, the sons of the grand old Sheik Abraham have been looking deep into the heart of nature and of man, and nourishing the life of the spirit in the darkness of their long night of adversity, as he nourished his beneath the stars of the Eastern sky."

The greatest Arabian philosopher of the Middle Ages, a teacher of Eationalism and of the eternity of matter. Many of his most distinguished disciples were Jews; and by Jews his works were translated, and transmitted throughout Europe. A strong current of materialistic infidelity flowed through the Jewish thought of those ages; and the physicians, the best of whom were nearly always Jews, were largely infected by it. The popular imagination linked together, not untruly, "Medicine, Arabianism, Aver-roesm, Astrology, Incredulity." The system of Averroes included, as well as the eternity of matter, " the evolution of the germ by its latent force, the impersonality of the intelligence, the immersion and re-absorption of the individual." Any one who cares to explore these " dry places" any farther, is referred to Kenans " Averroes et Averroesme." There was a feud of long standing between the Averroists and the Humanists (the philosophers and the men of letters), though the latter were often quite as open to the charge of incredulity.

"I have only heard Averroes and his school spoken of with hatred and aversion," Raymond said. " The Humanists–we are all Humanists here–have been always at war with the physicians and the rationalists."

"Especially when the Humanists are gentlemen, like Petrarch, and the physicians boors, like the rationalist doctor who offended his refined ear by the old vulgar jest, falsely attributed to Averroes, about the Three Impostors, Moses, Mahomet, and that Other whom I will not name, for never yet have I spoken irreverently of the greatest Jew that ever lived. Yet at bottom we are allies, fighting the same battles against the same foes. You yourself, Count Eaymond Chalcondyles, Grecian by birth, Latin by education, Artist by nature, Humanist by choice–tell me frankly, how do you regard holy mother Church?"

Eaymond answered with all the freedom his school allowed themselves when discussing such subjects, "Well, we laugh at her, but we like her on the whole. She is a fond, indulgent sort of mother, who gives us cakes and comfits, and shuts her eyes to our little peccadilloes, letting us fool her with a few set forms and soft speeches. We contrive to pay and to please, and so we are let alone."

"What if that fond, indulgent mother should some day change suddenly into an avenging fury, a Medea bathing hot hands in the blood of her own children? What if Giulios wild dream be true, and there sits on these seven hills, not the Mother and Mistress of Churches, but a woman dmnk with the blood of saints and martyrs, arrayed in purple and scarlet, decked with gold and jewels, and having a golden cup in her hand full of abominations and filthiness?"

"Gold and jewels, purple and scarlet, are here no doubt in abundance," Eaymond mused, " but"

–"But you are happy, and therefore you are tolerant; you have never suffered, and therefore you have never cursed or hated. Go to the homes of my people; go there as a Jew, and see their misery, their degradation–as surely the fruits of long ages of oppression as the poison berry of the nightshade grows from its bitter root–and you would hold other language, I dare to think. Measure the distance between David, Nehemiah, Daniel, the great Kabbis who made the Talmud, Moses Maimonides and his disciples, and that poor wretch I took yesterday from the dust of the Corso, who fawns on the hand that strikes him, and blesses and thanks the giver for the alms they fling him as they would a bone to a dog–and yet he is an elder, a in an of respectable family, of blameless life."

"But, Theodore, it is not fair to take the few, the heroes and philosophers of any race, and contrast them with the vulgar. Circumstances do not make all the difference between a King David and a vendor of old clothes."

"Fire does not make all the difference between gold and dross, but it shows it; for each behaves in it after its kind. We have walked for generations in the furnace heated seven times. It has made of us heroes, philosophers, martyrs–or at the other pole, pedlars, cheats, usurers, liars. For mark–you have forbidden us honour, arms, renown; you have barred our every path to glory and greatness, branded us with the brand of Cain, treated us as the offscouring of the earth. Had we been a poor weak race we should long ago have perished utterly off the face of the earth. But because we are strong to do and to suffer, because the life in us is vigorous and tenacious as that of the cedar on our native hills, against which the storms have beat in vain since Solomon planted it with the aid of the genii, we are here. We learned long ago that there are two things you cannot keep from us, gold and knowledge. The nobler spirits of our race have sought the one, the baser pursued the other. With what result? Oppressed, robbed, plundered a thousand times over, yet still, by fair means or by foul, the Jewish merchant and usurer spoils the souls of them that spoiled him, and grows rich at the gates of the impoverished Goim. Meanwhile, the Jewish thinker teaches philosophy to the few daring spirits amongst the Goim who care for philosophy at all; the Jewish physician takes charge of the health of his Holiness; t the Jewish astrologer sells his secrets to cardinals and bishops. No longer, as in earlier and perhaps happier days, do I quote the grand poetry of Isaiah and Ezekiel to prove the glorious future that awaits my people, but I appeal to the stern logic of facts, and I say that metal which has borne the furnace and the hammer as this has done is worthy to be forged hereafter into the two-edged sword of the conqueror."

So runs the legend.

t A fact. As late as the time of Leo X. the Popes physician was a Jew.

"That supposes," said Eaymond, "a hand to forge and a hand to wield the blade." He paused for a moment or two, listening rather anxiously to voices in the adjoining apartment, which was separated from theirs only by a curtain. " I was somewhat afraid," he said, "that

Manuel and what is your servants name?"

"Giulio; I thought I had told you." "That Manuel and Giulio might not agree, as Manuel, though an excellent fellow, has some awkward peculiarities. But I am reassured. I think he must be favouring your man with his whole history; I hear him talking of the wife and child he lost long ago in Constantinople, which he never does even to me."

"Giulio contrives to make every one talk without saying much himself."

"If he is a poor scholar, could we not get him a place here, and mend his fortunes?"

Theodore shook his head. " No, no; the best kindness you can do G-iulio is to ignore his existence. Truth is, Count Raymond–for I know a secret is safe with you–we Jews, being in everlasting revolt against the world that now is, which it is the fashion to call the Church, feel a natural sympathy with Christians who are rebels and outlaws too, Ishmaels, every mans hand against them, and theirs against every man. You remember Abrahams tenderness to Ishmael? " (Raymond remembered nothing about it, but that was no matter.) "Ever since the Holy Catholic Church has been mistress of the world, Ishmael has been going up and down through the lands of the Goim. His children have many names–Paulicians, Cathari, Manichasans, Fraticelli, Lollards, Albigenses, Waldenses, Insabbatici, Poor Men of Lyons. If they know their real opinions themselves, certainly no one else does. I dare say some of them believe quite as little as I–or you–others as much, or more, than their oppressors. But one thing they have all in common. Between them and the Power that sits on these seven hills is a hatred bottomless as the pit of Gehenna. At her hands they have endured, through long ages, horrors and agonies that make them my peoples rivals for the crown of sorrow. Yet they, like my people, survive. Booted out from one country by fire and sword, and strange forms of lingering death, straightway they spring up in another."

"Do you think, then, that they too have a future?"

"How can I tell? I may say, however, that one of them had almost made me a convert to his sect. He was a Manichee, one whose opinions Giulio most devoutly abhors, for rival heretics can hate like philosophers and curse uke friars. He found me in a dark and bitter hour, when first I gave up the faith learned at my mothers knee–the faith in Jehovah, the Lord of Hosts, the King of Israel."

Raymond looked surprised, if not distressed.

"Then you have given up that faith?" he said.

So great is the power of earnestness and reality, that Raymond had sometimes strengthened in his own heart the feeble flickering sentiment he called faith by a half-unconscious reference to his friends strong reliance upon the living God, the God of his fathers.

"Yes," Theodore answered; "I have looked deep into the things that are, and I see–nothing beyond. No one has ever seen anything. It is all guessing and dreaming."

"Well–perhaps–I dare say–you may be right," Raymond admitted, but rather with awakened curiosity and interest than with the sadness in which he ought to have spoken some of the saddest words that man can utter.

"I hold with the great Arab philosophers, and with those of my own race," Theodore went on, " that our senses tell us the truth, and all the truth. They show us nothing but matter, and there is nothing else. Out of its latent force everything is evolved, and to it everything returns."

"The Master would not go so far as that; but I think he is a Stoic, like the old Romans," Raymond said, with unabated cheerfulness.

"I am at rest now," continued Theodore. " Time was when I felt like a forsaken child, wailing in the dark for its mother. I forced myself to face the terrible truth. I went forth and looked upon the miseries of my people, and I said, No one cares, no one helps. Neither in heaven nor on earth is there justice, mercy, or pity. I saw that this creed of despair fitted the facts of the case, as a key the wards of the lock it is made for. If there is a God to do justice, then why is not justice done? Every miserable Jew tortured for the sake of his hard-won gold, every wretched heretic burned at the stake, is an argument for Averroes."

"Not necessarily. The suffering may be deserved–or something good may come out of it, we know not what or how," said Kay-mond, dimly guessing a flaw in his friends reasoning, yet not knowing where to touch it.

"It was a relief to catch at the Mani-chean compromise of the Two Principles, to believe in a good One, just, merciful, loving, but not necessarily omnipotent–always struggling with evil, destined perhaps in the end to be overcome by it." A momentary light flashed over the stern, sad face of Theodore, as he added, "I dreamed, and the dream was sweet, that I would fight for Him against evil, wrong, and cruelty, and at last fall with Him, if fate so willed it. Only a dream, the shadow of a shade! The Two Principles of Manes melt away and vanish into air, with all the other follies and fancies of our childhood, and the worlds. It is a terrible world, moving on, like some great resistless engine, without mind or will, but impelled by an iron necessity, from the germ out of which it sprang to the ruin I suppose it will crumble into. Out of that ruin, I suppose, other worlds will grow. What care I? A part of it myself, infinitely little, I must fulfil my destiny. When I die the universal will be joined to tha Universe, and the particular will return to the part, in the words of the great Joseph ben Juda, the pupil of Maimonides."

Both were silent, and in the silence the voice of Giulio from the other room reached their ears distinctly.

"In my Fathers house are many mansions: if it were not so, I would have told you. I go to prepare a place for you. And if I go and prepare a place for you, I will come again, and receive you unto myself; that where I am, there ye may be also. And whither I go ye know, and the way ye know."

Bach looked in the face of the other; neither said a word, but tears were gathering in the eyes of Theodore.

A loud knocking at the door broke the silence with such startling suddenness that both sprang to their feet. But Raymond recovered his self-possession in a moment.

"Some of my friends are playing a carnival trick upon me," he said. " They know you are here, and that we are almost alone, as I gave Giacopo a holiday. Dont mind them." Then, raising his voice, "Stay, Manuel, I will go to the door myself."

Which he did; and was immediately laid hold upon by strong arms, and pinioned. He struggled desperately, half laughing, half breathless.

"Hands off! This is past a joke," he cried. "Agathocles, I know the shape of your hand."

"Let me caution you, signor, not to name any of your acquaintances. It may do them a serious injury," said a person who seemed to be the captain of the armed band, now rapidly filling the room.

It was an age of violence, and Rome was often the theatre of wild deeds of private vengeance. Could Raymond have offended some Colonna or Orsini? No;–for he had never made an enemy, so far as he knew, and the nobles of late had always respected the scholars. No;–for these men bore the Papal arms and uniform.

Theodore, in his doctors robe, advanced to demand an explanation, but was rudely thrust aside; as was Manuel, in spite of his desperate struggles to aid his master. But Giulio succeeded in making his voice heard for a moment.

"Possibly there is some mistake, signori," he said. " Whom does your warrant command you to arrest?"

"Count Raymond Chalcondyles," was the ready answer. " You may go, you others. The sooner the better."

Raymond began to comprehend that he was a prisoner–the prisoner of his Holiness. But of what his offence could be, he had not the faintest conception.

"What am I accused of? " he asked.

"Our business is to be silent; yours to deliver up to us, without delay, all books, letters, or other writings this house may contain belonging to Messer Pomponius Laetus. And see that you conceal nothing."

For the first time in his life Raymond stood face to face with peril, possibly with death. It proved the temper of his soul. Drawing himself up to his full height, he said, with a flash of scorn, "Find the masters writings as you may; you shall have no help from me. Nor shall you find aught unworthy of a sage or a scholar."

"We shall soon see that, young gentleman."

Raymond was bound, and closely watched by some of the band, whilst others seized books and broke open desks and boxes.

"I am his servant, surely you will let me go with him," pleaded Manuel in agony.

–" Go to the evil one, with your leavened wafer, you accursed Greek schismatic! " was the urbane reply.

Theodore, much more adroit, slipped some gold into the hand of the captain, a German mercenary. " Let me say two words to my friend," he whispered.

"Do not use violence with the prisoner," said that gentleman, a good deal mollified. "Allow his friend to approach him and to receive his instructions."

Theodore drew near to Eaymond, who, said to him hurriedly, in Greek, "Send Manuel to Venice at once–at once. Bid him warn the Master not to return, but to conceal himself. Some one must have slandered him to the Pope; though wherefore, or in what manner, I have not the least idea. I understand nothing about this affair. Let Manuel also tell my mother what has happened; but with management, so as not to alarm her. And you, Theodore, go yourself and relate everything to Cardinal Bessarion."

"That will I. Remember, there are countrymen of mine in the Popes palace–everywhere. We will do all we can. God be with thee, dear friend."

Words that, from the lips of Theodore, could have meant no more than an assurance of friendship and affection. But in that meaning they were utterly sincere.

A few minutes more, and Theodore and Griulio stood face to face in gloomy silence, the floor around them strewn with rifled chests, damaged books, and broken furniture. A little apart, Manuel wept and wailed, wringing his hands in the bitterness of his anguish. " How shall I ever hold up my face to my lady? Not to speak of my blessed master and lord, who is with the saints in Paradise. Holy St. Nicholas of Myra have pity on the boy! Blessed St. John of Antioch deliver him out of the hands of these pitiless Latins, who are as bad as infidel Turks! Aiao! Aiao!–I knew harm would come of it–we came to live here on the fifth day of the month; on the fifth day also Signor Pomponio left us; five letters we have received from him, and five times "

"Cease thy useless lamentations! " cried Theodore, seizing his arm without ceremony, as he was about to tear his hair and beard. " Better serve thy young lord like a man than cry for him like a girl. Giulio, my friend, run to my lodging and bring me the casket thou kupwest of. Slip on this domino of Count Raymonds, so niayest thou pass for some belated reveller. Manuel, find me an ink-horn–here are paper and pens; then put on thy sword and cloak ready for a journey."

Giulio started on his errand, while Manuel, subdued by the doctors air of authority, iound the ink-horn, and disappeared to obey the rest of his orders.

The modern Greeks think five a particularly unlucky number.

Theodore wrote a hurried letter to his father, referring him to Manuel for details of what had happened, and imploring him to use all his influence on behalf of Raymond. Might not his financial dealings enable him to put the screw upon some personages very near his Holiness? After disposing of the affair that just then filled all his thoughts he added hastily–since confidential messengers between Bome and Venice must be made the most of, being few and costly–" I arrived here the day before yesterday, after a prosperous journey. I have already fulfilled the commission you gave me. I repaired to the Palazzo Porcaro, and having represented that I came from you, was fortunate enough to procure an interview with the Signorina Viola. She is much changed since I used to know her at Venice. I gave your message, and she answered that she. wished to have the things belonging to her grandfather, which you hold in your keeping, sent hither to her. It were well to send them by Manuel when he returns. They say she—-

Here Theodore paused, as if uncertain, and looking up saw that Manuel stood by his side ready equipped for the journey. So he brought his letter to a close, merely adding those expressions of filial respect which were customary at the time, and which he could use in all sincerity.

The casket Giulio was charged to bring contained his stock of ready money, and that he gave to Manuel, telling him to make his way on foot for the first stage to avoid suspicion, and then to hire horses for the rest of the journey. " Go in peace," he said, " and be thy watchword Speed and silence."

Meanwhile Eaymond watched the breaking of the day in a gloomy cell within the massy walls of the Castle of St. Angelo. He sat idle, almost stupefied, his eyes fixed on the iron bars of his little window, his mind filled with amazement and per plexity, rather than with alarm or distress. If he felt fear it was for his beloved and venerated Master, far more than for himself.

The persecution of the members of the Boman Academy by Paul II. is an historical fact. The blow seems to have fallen upon them quite as suddenly and unexpectedly as has been represented above. They were arrested during the carnival of 1468, imprisoned in the Castle of St. Angelo, and put to the torture. Platina, one of the victims, has left on record a graphic account of his sufferings, and of those of his companions. The Pope suspected them, or pretended to suspect them, of a conspiracy against his life, but he failed to extort any evidence of its existence. He then brought forward a charge of heresy, which was not easy either to establish or to refute. Nothing definite could be proved against them; but the Pope was no doubt justified in his conviction that the spirit of their teaching was inimical to that of the Church.

CHAPTER XII.

DARK DAYS.

JHE great crises of life usually come upon us by surprise–to-day vague uneasiness, to-morrow sharp anxiety, the next day overwhelming sorrow. Thus Raymond, who was at first disposed to regard his imprisonment as a fleeting cloud, "like a mans hand," soon found that " the heaven was dark with clouds and wind, and there was a great rain." He was treated with a degree of harshness that moved his indignant surprise; his narrow cell was furnished only with the barest necessaries, his food was coarse and scanty, and his feet were fettered. " What have I done to be treated thus? " he asked his jailors, but only received surly and evasive answers. When, however, he requested permission to communicate with his friends, he was vouchsafed the information, anything but reassuring, that they were, all of them, in the same position as himself.

"What! " he cried, " have they taken the Master?"

"If you mean that baptized heathen and heretic Pomponio Laeto, his Holiness has not caught him yet; but he will have him soon enough, and call him to account for his crimes," said the warder.

"Keep a civil tongue, varlet, when you talk of scholars and gentlemen," returned the angry and imprudent prisoner. " Corpo di Bacco! Had a knight or noble dared to call the Master heathen and heretic it were worth measuring swords over. If I had my sword! " he broke off sadly.

"Very well, my fine young gentleman," the warder retorted spitefully. " You will sing to another tune when you are put on the pulley, like your learned and accomplished friend Signor Platina. See if you do not call your master heathen and heretic yourself, ay, and conspirator against the life of his Holiness."

"That will I do never–never!" cried Eaymond, his cheek, which had paled at the mention of the torture, flushing with proud, heroic resolution.

Yet as soon as the warder locked the door and left him to his solitude he flung himself on the mat that served him as a bed, and wept and sobbed like a child. " Mother, mother," he murmured through his tears, " do you know of all this?"

Wonder at last came to his aid, softening his grief and terror, or at least serving to divert his mind. "What can it all mean?" he said aloud, for in his loneliness he found it a kind of relief thus to utter his thoughts. " We have done nothing unlawful–nothing. The Master has no thought beyond his Latin books, his pupils, his antiquarian researches. How he can have offended his Holiness it is impossible to conceive. Some one must have invented foul slanders against him and all of us. Who, I marvel, are the victims of this abominable malice beside the Master and myself? And Platina, that accomplished scholar, the glory of our academy, to whom we all looked up with such reverence? Who else? Campano? Molza? Sannazaro? Porcaro? Ah, Porcaro! " (the name sent a sudden thrill of pain through every nerve, making his lip quiver and his tears flow once more). "Well, thank God, nothing can touch her. There beats not on earth a heart so base as to injure such as her." Then, after a long shuddering sigh, "Better name no names in the hearing of that scoundrel of a turnkey, it might do harm. Heaven help me! I know not what to do, or to leave undone."

This was true; Eaymond had passed his young life hitherto in an atmosphere of freedom and security. He had yet to learn his first lesson in the mournful science of the oppressed, the lesson of silence. He was like a wild creature who has never seen the face of the hunter; frank, unsuspecting, fearless, he would have played with the very instruments of death.

"Conspirator against the life of his Holiness?" he repeated the warders words. "As much as against the life of Julius Caesar. Certainly the Master often praised Brutus, talked of him as the deliverer of his country, wished such men for Romans now. Could the Holy Father have taken offence at such words as those? Impossible. Heathen and heretic? What is a heretic?–heretics are burned alive. But assuredly we are no heretics, we scholars. We believe–I am sure I dont know what we believe! " said Raymond, in utter perplexity, as he rose from his seat and began to pace the narrow bounds of his dungeon as well as his fettered feet would allow him.

It was quite true that scholars such as Pomponius Laetus and Platina were not likely to go beyond vague sentimental praises of freedom and antiquity; and perhaps some rash glorification of the shade of Brutus. The Pope had little to fear from them as rebels. But was he, after all, mistaken in treating them as heretics? He would have sent Giulio to the stake for calling the wafer a piece of bread and refusing his reverence to the finger bone of St. Cosmo. Who could tell whether Pomponius Laetus believed at all in the Godhead of Him whom the wafer represents, or in the continued existence of St. Cosmo, or of any saint, beyond the grave? Yet the general tenure of the Churchs practice condemns the severity of Paul. Eome, as a rule, wages war with the living, not with the dead. Mere scepticism, Eome thinks, is death; and death is harmless because it is powerless. But is it? Does not the putrefaction of the grave engender poison gases, which slay their tens of thousands? Perhaps, after all, the grim fanatic who filled the papal chair had eyes to see the true interests of the Papacy. Yet he ought to have been content with the banishment, or the imprisonment, of the heads of the academy. Nothing can remove the stain left upon his memory by atrocious cruelties inflicted on a band of innocent, generous youths, whose only offence was their zeal for ancient literature and their attachment to their teachers.

When another and rather more civil warder brought Eaymond his evening meal of black bread and beans, he ventured to ask, "What physician attends the prisoners? " He had been thinking in the meantime that it might be possible to communicate with Theodore through a brother in the craft, not improbably also a brother in blood.

"Are you ill? " the warder inquired.

"Not at all. I ask from curiosity."

"Dr. Levi Volterra,"–the name confirmed Kaymonds hope that he was a Jew. "But you are likely to make his acquaintance soon enough, poor lad. You are to be examined to-morrow." With this grim hint he took his leave.

Kaymond pushed the food away with a look of disgust, and threw himself once more on his mat. " I will try to sleep and forget my misery for a little while," he thought. Sleep, thus wooed, does not often prove propitious, yet at last he did fall into an uneasy slumber.

A sound awakened him suddenly, a sound that he had heard before, but disregarded, in happy ignorance of its terrible import,–a cry, faint as if coming from a distance, yet fearfully distinct and shrill, It was repeated again, and yet again. He started up. Cold drops stood upon his forehead. He listened, spellbound, almost holding his breath. Every sound made him shiver from head to foot; yet with the fascination of horror he would not allow himself to miss one. " Hodie tibi, eras mihi," he thought, and shuddered. Would those cries never cease?

Platina, himself a sufferer, says that " the Castle of St. Angelo resembled the bull of Phalaris, resounding day and night with the cries and groans of these innocent. young men."

At last there was silence–blessed silence, Eaymond thought at first. Then he began to wonder, was it the silence of death with the victim? " Oh, that I could pray," he thought, "for him and for myself!" He threw himself on his knees, but no words would come. Then it occurred to him to repeat an Ave, and he ran over a dozen hurriedly, from a blind impulse of terror.

But he rose uncomforted, and with a kind of self-contempt. " What have I been doing? "he asked himself. "I desire that God would help some poor friend of mine in his misery, and I have been gabbling over and over again Hail, Mary, full of grace, the Lord is with thee.–Oh, God, help me! Help us all in this our hour of bitter need!–But will He help? Does He hear? Is He there at all?–Every one in trouble says prayers, so I suppose there is some use in them. Even Sannazaro, scoffer though he is, crossed himself and said a prayer when we were caught in that thunderstorm in the Borghese Gardens.–Ah, happy days!–My mother prays and so does Manuel. But what shall I say? Pater Noster, that means our Father. In my Fathers house are many mansions. Who said those words?–I ought to strengthen myself by thinking of the ancients, that is what the Master would tell me, were he here. There was Mutius Scsevola, who thrust his hand into the fire; Regulus, who endured so many tortures for the sake of his country; Anax- archus"

But it was in vain that Raymond tried to fix his thoughts upon these elevating examples of fortitude. He felt like a child in an agony of grief over a dead mother, to whom some one offers a toy by way of consolation. These were but toys with which his fancy sported in hours of ease, in real and terrible anguish they had no help to give him. The more he endea voured to meditate upon them, the more empty and meaningless they seemed to grow; until at last they presented no image to his mind beyond that of the letters that composed their names, written upon parchment by the Masters hand.

He was still vainly endeavouring to draw from his stores of memory something more suited to his need, when he heard the key grate once again in his prison door. A light flashed in, and the jailors voice summoned him to arise and follow.

"To-morrow–he said to-morrow," Eay-mond exclaimed in an agitated voice as he started to his feet.

"It does not signify what he said. The Commissary of his Holiness desires your attendance."

Eaymond summoned all his manliness. " Give me a moment," he asked, " that I may arrange my dress."

"That is but due respect for his Excellency," returned the jailor. "But hasten."

Eaymond smoothed his fair hair, sorely disordered by his night of agony, and made some trifling changes in his apparel; an evidence of courage and self-respect not lost upon the jailor. But he also contrived, while standing with his back to that functionary, to take out something unperceived by him, and to slip it under his mat. For he feared that–if the worst came–rude hands might meddle with his clothing. What he concealed so carefully was only a little silken bag, containing a small gold reliquary and part of a childs silver bracelet.

CHAPTER XIII.

TRUE TO THE MASTER.

1 And soon all vision waxeth dull;
Men whisper, He is dying;
We cry no more Be pitiful;
We have no strength for crying.
No strength! No need! Then, soul of mine,
Look up and triumph rather:
Lo! in the depths of Gods Divine
The Son adjures the Father,
Be pitiful, 0 God!"

lyMOND underwent a searching examination, turning first upon the alleged conspiracy against the life of the Pope, and then upon his Masters opinions, practices, and mode of life. With regard to the conspiracy, his answers were clear, unwavering, and explicit. No clever cross-questioning could entrap him, no threat of torture could shake his testimony. The Master was innocent.

But on the subject of the opinions taught in the academy he held his ground less firmly, perhaps because he knew it less thoroughly. He owned that the academicians had been accustomed to observe certain heathen festivals, especially that caued the Palilia, and that of the Foundation of Rome; but he maintained that they did so merely as antiquarians, and for amusement. In the same manner he explained their practice of giving themselves heathen names borrowed from the ancients; he protested earnestly that it did not arise from any intention of renouncing their baptism. When pressed to admit that Pomponius in his teaching had called in question certain primary doctrines of the Faith, he said that these speculations were merely theses, put forward in the schools for the sake of argument, and that " the Master" (as he was careful to style Pom ponius even then) had always denounced and detested Averroesm and Rationalism. He said that he himself had been a Greek in his childhood, but that when he came to Venice he had conformed to the Latin ritual, and since then had attended Mass, confessed occasionally, and lived in all things like a good Catholic. But he owned, though with some hesitation, that he could not think it a mortal sin to communicate in the leavened wafer, since his noble ancestors, now with God, had done so for many generations. It is difficult for us to understand the condition of mind that made this seem a serious matter to Raymond, while to have entertained speculative doubts upon the very existence of God was. but a trifling peccadillo.

He was remanded to his cell, with impressive warnings to be more explicit next time, and appalling threats of what would follow should he fail to satisfy his examiners.

Threats which were destined never to be fulfilled. Raymond was never doomed to learn " the dread mystery of pain " on the rack or the pulley. This exemption was the more singular, because of all the pupils of Pomponius he might be supposed to know him the most intimately, since for years he had enjoyed his hospitality and dwelt beneath his roof. But it happened, fortunately for him, that the Papal Commissary and Inquisitor, Sanga of Chiozza, was at once a voluptuary and a virtuoso, with tastes, both fashionable and expensive, for "horses and brown Greek MSS.," and other delights " of the flesh and of the mind." These led to pecuniary embarrassment, and that to Jewish usurers. He owed a large sum to Benedetto, the Jewish banker at Venice; and Benedettos son was now at hand to whisper that if his friend were too harshly dealt with, certain moneys would be urgently required, and must be forthcoming at once. Had his creditor been a Roman Jew the Commissary might have laughed at his threats; but the Re-public knew how to make her citizens respected abroad. The Commissary, like his master the Pope, was by birth a citizen of the Venetian Eepublic, and therefore anxious to stand well with the Signory; moreover he was aware that it was seldom safe or convenient to defraud a merchant of Venice. The Island City might have boasted, like Nuremberg, that her "hand reached every land."

Had Eaymond but known all this! Perhaps the fear that every day, every hour almost, might bring the dreaded agony, was even worse than its actual infliction, once for all. If it had come it would have passed, and probably have been succeeded by the inspiriting reaction that follows having faced and borne the worst. But as it was, spring melted into summer–the sultry Eoman summer–and brought no change, no relief. All day the pitiless sun blazed down on the scorching leads of the Castle, and directly beneath these was the cell in which Eaymond languished. Sleep was impossible, and the coarse food given him he could scarcely touch. His high spirit was well-nigh crushed at last. When one day he was told that " the Master " too was in prison–delivered up by the Venetian Senate into the. hands of the pitiless Pope–he wept long and helplessly, like a child. But the next visit of the warder found him calm and tearless. " I wish," he said, " to ask-for a confessor. I think my sorrows will soon be over now."

The official, who happened to be the more humane of the two that waited on him, answered kindly enough, "It is not a priest you should ask for, but a physician. I will get permission for Dr. Levi to visit you, and then it will be time enough to see about the confessor."

It was true that he needed a physician; he had tossed all night on his mat, burning and gasping for air, but he was shivering now, even in the scorching heat of his cell.

In a happy hour for him the warder unlocked the door, and admitted, for a first visit out of many, a brisk little Jew, with wrinkled face and bushy eyebrows, small piercing black eyes, and black hair sprinkled with grey. Dr. Levi Volterra was a specimen of his race very different from Theodore or his father. Keen, shrewd, covetous, unscrupulous but not unkindly, cautious but determined, and above all persevering, he was just the man to resolve upon success and to achieve it. If, with him, success meant nothing but well-filled money bags, it was perhaps the fault of those who had denied the Jew all the other prizes of life. He was physician, astrologer, fortune-teller, and upon occasion a dozen things besides, more or less creditable, but always lucrative. He had embraced the Christian faith after serious deliberation. " I shall lose the good-will of my own people, but I shall gain that of the Goim, and they are the strongest," such were the arguments that decided him. He never forgot that he had to make the fortune, not of Dr. Levi Volterra alone, but also of a black-eyed Jewish wife and a goodly number of thriving olive-branches.

To such a man Theodores overtures were as the voice of the charmer. " Charm he never so wisely " Dr. Levi would not endanger his place, not to say his head; but anything that could be done with safety for Kaymond and his fellow-prisoners he would do. Already he pitied the persecuted students, and had shown them such trifling kindnesses as lay in his power.

Through his agency Theodore was now able to send messages of hope and encouragement to Eaymond, and to provide better food for him. The doctor contrived also that he should be relieved from his fetters, and held out promises of soon being able to effect his removal to a more airy apartment. Under this treatment Eaymonds strength revived a little, and the low fever that had prostrated him gradually passed away.

It was a sign of returning life that he began to make little requests of the kindly doctor. To write to his mother, and to send the letter through Theodores agency, was his first desire. This being obtained, he asked for news of his companions, then for a few books, and at length, much to the doctors surprise, for " a bit of clay." " Soft clay, such as they use for moulding figures," he explained.

"You shall have it," said the doctor, smiling. " It is a good plan to occupy your hands. But hark you, Count Kaymond, try no tricks with it on your own account, such as hiding billets, for example. My good friend and brother, Dr. Theodore Benedetto, manages all that with me, and any ill-advised interference on your part might bring us both to the pulley."

Eaymond satisfied him on this point. "I only want to amuse myself modelling the things I think of as I sit here all day die," he said; and the doctor, on his next visit, produced the clay from beneath his robe.

One evening shortly afterwards Eaymond was employed upon it, when both the warders entered his cell and ordered him to accompany them.

"You are to share the apartment of one of your companions; the doctor has obtained this great favour for you both," he was told in answer to his inquiries.

Eaymonds heart throbbed quick and fast as he accompanied the warders. While the door of his new prison was being unbarred he waited impatiently, expecting the next moment to clasp some beloved fellow-student in a brothers embrace. But no arms were opened to receive him, no voice spoke a greeting. At first he thought the cell was tenantless. He was mistaken. There was a low, faint murmur of his name, and at length through the quickly falling twilight he discerned a wasted form, a pallid, deathlike face. In a moment he was kneeling beside the mat on which his fellow-prisoner lay. "My Callimachus, is it thou? Ah, carissimo!"

"Call me by the name my mother used; I have done with those vain heathen fancies now," said the dying youth, for such he truly was.

"Dearest Agostino, is it thus we meet? How you must have suffered! " said Eay-mond, almost weeping.

"Yes, it has been bitter–bitter. But the worst is over now. You will find some wine on the table, Kaymond. Give it me, I pray you. For my strength is going, and I want to talk to you while I can. I have so much to say."

Eaymond found the wine and gave it. But the joy of seeing a friendly face and grasping a friendly hand did more than wine to revive the failing powers of Cam-pano. For a brief season the flickering spark of life flashed into a flame. With Eaymonds arm around him and his head pillowed on Eaymonds shoulder he was able to converse, in a low tone indeed, but without pain or discomfort.

"You will be saved, Eaymond; I am sure of it," he said. "You must tell my father and my mother that they have my last thoughts and prayers. Tell them, too, that I did not disgrace our ancient name. I said no word that was false, and–all through–I was true to the Master."

Eaymond whispered some words of hope, but Campano shook his head. " I have done with all that," he said. " Even the wish to live is gone from me. I used to long for the sunshine, the blue sky, the familiar faces–for the free boyish life in my fathers home, and, better still, our happy student days. Dost remember the Palilia, Eaymond, and the sport we had then? Ah, but it was not well done to forget the good God as we did in those days."

"If we erred, we have been sorely punished," said Eaymond bitterly. " What had you done, my Agostino–you that were ever blameless, more than most of us–to deserve the cruel anguish they have made you suffer?"

"Do not let us think of our deservings. No help comes that way. Let us think of the Cross, Eaymond, and of what He suffered there. That was worse than the rack."

"I have tried such thoughts," said Ray-mond, " and I have found no comfort in them. It does not take the bitterness out of my pain to think of the pain endured by Anaxarchus, or Regulus, or Christ."

"Regulus–or Christ! Mio caro, they are quite different. Regulus was an old Eoman, dead and buried long ago; Christ is the Saviour."

"True. But what then?"

"Cant you see? That cross was borne for us. And He who bore it lives still for us–to help and save us."

"You have become devout, my Agostino. Doubtless you have seen the priest?"

"Yes, and he has comforted me. Tomorrow I am to communicate–he has promised it. He assures me the good God will accept my repentance, late though it is. But better than even his words (good words though they were) was this letter," and with feeble hand he drew from beneath his pillow a closely written sheet of paper, aad showed it to Raymond.

"I think I know the writing," said he, looking at it with interest. " Whose is it?"

"The strange thing is, I know not. There is no name. I know only that the writer is a friend of Dr. Theodores, who has shown us all so much kindness, and that he sent it to me through Dr. Levi. Some good priest or friar doubtless. But whoever he is, night and day I pray God to bless him. Keep it, my Eaymond, and read it for thyself–when I–have done with it.

"It came to me in the darkest hour, when first I felt that God–for whom we cared nothing in the old days–was strong and terrible, and angry with me. Every nerve in my body, quivering with intolerable pain, told me how dreadful the Popes anger could be. And, after all, he is but a man. But Gods anger! Christs, the Judge of all men! When I tried to look up, I could see nothing but that awful Face on the cross, could hear nothing but that terrible voice, Depart from me, ye cursed, into everlasting fire.

"I once heard a friar preach on that text, and I mocked him, Raymond–mocked him! I laughed at the poor ignorant people who wept and wailed aloud, and lashed themselves with scourges in the darkened church. Now all came back to me–the cries and groans and sobbing, and the mournful chant that rose above them all–Dies irae; Dies illa3. The priest told me God might forgive–might–if the blessed Mother and all the holy saints were to intercede for me. But this letter says that He Himself is far tenderer, far more compassionate, than they. Think of it,–the great Son of God more tender than sweet Mother Mary! See, His own words are here. How He received poor sinners who came to Him while on earth; how He has promised to cast out none that come–no, I thought, not even me; if I cry to Him out of the depths, He will hear and answer me. And He has. That Face on the cross, as I see it now, is not stern and awful. It is the Face of One who loves me. It shines on me the long night through with infinite pity and tenderness; it will shine on me through the longer night that is gathering around me now.

"I wonder what death will be like? What comes after?–It does not matter. I can never lose the sight of that Pace, never feel afraid while He is there."

Again those words occurred to Eaymond, "In my Fathers house are many mansions–I go to prepare a place for you." He repeated them aloud. "I think," he said, "they must be His words, for He is the Son of God. And if I go away, I will come again and receive you unto myself, that where I am, there ye may be also."

"Unto myself, "Agostino repeated, slowly but with deep feeling. "It is not hard to go to Him. Not harder than it would be to go home out of this dungeon. Nay, it is going home."

This was the only conversation the re united friends were able to hold. Agostinos strength, which had seemed for a moment to return, ebbed again so quickly that

Kaymond, who spent the night in ministering to him with the tenderness of a brother, prayed the warder, when he came in the morning, to send at once both for the physician and the priest.

The physician could do but little; and as the ministrations of the priest required that he should be left alone with his penitent, Eaymond, to his great sorrow, was removed to an adjoining cell. As he stooped down to kiss the pale forehead of his friend his tears fell fast upon it.

Agostino contrived to slip into his hand the strangers letter. " Take it," he whispered,–" safe with you. Addio, carissimo."

Eaymond would have lingered still, but the doctor hurried him away. " Come, signor," he said, " you shall return again; I pledge my word for it."

A promise kept to the ear, but broken to the heart. When, two hours afterwards, Eaymond was led back to the cell, the solemn presence of death was there.

Contrary to the usual custom, no priestly watcher sat beside the bed; but four tapers had been lit, and burned in the daylight with a pale and ghastly gleam. Eaymond felt the loneliness, the desolation, of the scene. Yet there was comfort in weeping over his friend without the restraint of a witnessing eye or ear, and the tears he shed seemed to bring a soothing influence with them. A calm, half listless, but half hopeful too, stole over his troubled spirit; perhaps it was a shadow of the peace that sealed the pallid features of the dead.

One of the academicians, Agostino Campano, a young nobleman of high expectations and of the most promising talents and character, died in the Castle of St. Angelo from the effects of the torture.

CHAPTER XIV.

CHAINS BROKEN.

IJOUNT Eaymond Chalcondyles, are you a brave man?"

Eaymond rose up from before his dead," and with some surprise on his sorrowful face, met the searching gaze of Dr. Levi Volterra. " Why do you ask?"

"Because if you are," said the doctor in a whisper from which he could not banish all signs of agitation, " you may be a free man by the mornings light."

Eaymonds heart throbbed with a strong sudden bound; his eyes shone through their quivering tears.

"Were I the veriest coward upon earth," he said, "I could dare and suffer all things for that hope."

"Be quiet then. Sit down and listen to me. I am running a terrible risk for your sake, young gentleman–a terrible risk."

"There are those who will reward you nobly, and God and the saints will bless you."

"Che! che! we will hope so," said the little physician–who, of course, had not accepted the perilous role he was about tc play without large stipulations for protection and compensation. His family were already on their way to Venice, and he himself was soon to follow, with the assurance of a good place and a handsome competence from the influence and liberality of the Benedettos. " But I put myself apart–quite apart,." he continued, "I think of you alone at present. Does not the unwonted absence of the priest from the chamber of death surprise you?"

"Nay, it revolts me," Eaymond answered with warmth; "that the body of my friend should lie unwatched and untended seems a bitter and grievous insult, worthy of the cruelty that brought him to his death."

"Do not blame the poor priest. He was overcome by his trying duties, and felt faint; so he asked me for a cordial, and I gave him one."

"Well?"

"He is on his own bed now, nearly as helpless as the dead on his. I can give you the same, if you like."

"Heaven forbid!"

"Oh, as for that, I have not harmed him. He will be well enough to-morrow. I am no poisoner, Count Eaymond; but I wanted him out of the way for a few hours. Now listen. The kinsfolk of that poor young gentleman have made their humble suit to the Pope, that his remains may be given up to them, and the Pope has granted their prayer–most graciously." There was a whole world of hate and irony in the emphasis flung upon the last words.

But Raymond made, no response. His spirit had sunk below the point where invectives give relief. He only said mournfully–

"Oh, what a home-coming! God comfort his poor mother. But are his kinsfolk then in the city?"

"His father is here; and his hand is with us in this business. Count Raymond, you must take the place of the dead in his coffin, he yours on yonder couch."

Raymond started, and his pale face took a yet deeper pallor.

"Oh, not that!" he cried. "How could I take from that mourning father the sad consolation of looking once more upon the face of the dead, and from my friend his chance of an honourable and Christian burial?"

"Better so, than for thy mother to mourn as his to-day. Be reasonable, Count Raymond. I tell you the father of your friend has given his willing consent to the plan; and as for him–can it matter so much, after all? The priest tells me lie has made a most edifying end, like a saint or martyr in fact; and there will be masses in abundance said for the repose of his soul."

Eaymond turned, and stood in silence, looking at the dead.

"If I but knew," he said at last, " that the touch of no rude careless hand would profane what was once Agostino Campano."

"You may trust. When the authorities discover what is done, they will lay the remains reverently enough within the fortress. Popes may be infallible, but they are not immortal; and men less shrewd than the governor of the castle may reflect that times change, and that the victims of one day are the martyrs of the next."

Eaymond heard little more than the opening words of this speech. His soul was holding converse with itself. Life looked beautiful to him: the wine was red, and gave its colour in the cup, and moved itself aright–he could not push it aside untasted from his lips.

"I will try your plan," he said at last.

"That is well, Count Eaymond."

"I think he would wish it, could he choose," Eaymond pursued, still looking at the dead. " True friend, thy life was given for the master; thy grave is given for me."

"More true to him you call the master than the master has been to himself," said the Jewish doctor sharply. " Your great Pomponius Laetus has written to the Pope, explaining and excusing everything, and imploring mercy in terms the most humble."

"It is false–I do not believe a word of it," said Eaymond with a flash of the old enthusiasm; which, nevertheless, was waning and paling gradually, as all passions, not intertwisted with the very roots of a mans being, are sure to do under bitter and protracted suffering.

"That is just as you please," said the doctor, satisfied with his success in bringing the colour to his patients cheek and the fire to his eye. Indignation is a good stimulant, although, as with other stimulants, there is danger of reaction.

"Now, Count Raymond, let me explain to you the details of our plan, as they have been carefully elaborated by Dr. Theodore and myself, with the assistance of Dr. Theodores invaluable servant. Perils and plotting seem to be that mans native element; he is like a fox of the mountains, who has baffled the pursuers so often that he is an adept in every turn and doubling, and the more daring the game the better he likes it." (Dr. Levi, himself a timid man, admired daring exceedingly.) "When the warders come at midnight to remove the dead; Count Raymond lies on his pallet in yonder corner; he has been ill and is sleeping with exhaustion; I have covered him carefully with his own mantle, and beg them not to disturb him. I volunteer my aid in their mournful office, which they are certain to regard with the greatest repugnance, like all your Eomans of the lower class. Probably with very scant and careless help from them, I lay the body in the coffin they have brought. If you have ever seen a Eoman coffin, you know it is at best a coa, rse, ill-made shell; and Gaulio shall contrive that this one be sufficiently ill-made to admit the air–since a living man must breathe. It will be delivered up to the becchini at the gate of the castle, as they could not be permitted to enter here. Giulio himself makes one of them; but the others are not in the secret, nor are the Frati who will attend with tapers, as it would not be safe to intrust it to so many. The coffin duly laid upon the bier, and the velvet pall thrown over it as usual, the mournful procession will wind its way through the silent streets to the Church of Santa Maria in Trastevere."

In ordinary cases this is done by the lecchini, or bearers, persons of the lowest class, who are hired for the occasion. But it is impossible to suppose that such would have been allowed to enter the prison.

"Where Stefano Porcaro lies buried?" said Eaymond. " Ah! I fear nothing there!"

"You need not. The men of Trastevere are less degenerate than the rest–old Eomans, so at least they call themselves, and perhaps they have a spark of the old fire in them yet. The church once reached, you are safe. The cura is a kinsman of the Porcari, and what you call a Humanist. He and Dr. Theodore will await you there, and open the door of your narrow prison; and to-morrow you will see the sun rise."

Words which threw Eaymond into a dream of rapture, from which, however, the practical doctor quickly recalled him. " We have enough to do between this and midnight," he said, "but our first duty is to strengthen you. Here are bread, meat, and wine. Do justice, I pray you, to the hospitality of his Holiness, for you are not likely to enjoy it again."

Thus exhorted, Eaymond tried to eat; but his was the courage of the highly-strung nervous organization, not that of the hard phlegmatic one–and he failed. He drank some wine, however, and then silently assisted the doctor in the arrangements rendered necessary by their plan. Allowing for an interval of rest, which the doctor insisted upon his taking while he watched by his side, still before midnight all was ready; the dead lay in the place of the living, the living in that of the dead.

At last the great clock of the castle sounded the midnight hour, and with extraordinary punctuality the door was unlocked, and the warders entered with their solemn burden. Raymond heard every sound, but of course saw nothing. He lay perfectly still, his limbs composed into the closest simulation of the rigidity of death possible to the living. The warders disliked the sight and the touch of the dead quite as much as the doctor expected, so that he succeeded admirably in performing the only part of his task that he had regarded with apprehension. He took care to leave the castle with the funeral procession–and for the last time.

For Raymond, the horror of the two hours that followed was only rendered endurable by the sweet hope of freedom. He learned the meaning of " darkness that might be felt." In vain he tried to occupy his thoughts by listening to the hoarse, monotonous chant of the Frati, "Miserere Domine," their rough, careless, unmusical voices only exasperated him. Then he sought to divert his mind by encouraging all sorts of vague, trivial, irrelevant fancies. Some of these connected themselves with the letter Agostino had given him; and which he read during his mournful interval of waiting in the empty cell. The penmanship, rather than the matter, occupied his thoughts; he was perplexed by its resemblance to that of Giacomo, the painter friend of his boyhood, who had written to him once or twice since he came to Rome. Only a morbid fancy (so far as he knew) could identify GKacomo with the unknown correspondent of Agostino. Still, those capitals and final flourishes were, to say the least of it, remarkable. There was a kind of harmony too between Giacomos picture of the compassionate Saviour leading the blind man out of the city that He might restore his sight (how well he remembered that picture! was it finished yet? he wondered;) and this writers eloquent delineation of His infinite love and pity, the love of a Man for men. Could it indeed be true that a human heart was throbbing within the blaze of the unapproachable light? That the Cross meant tenderness, not terror? Hitherto he had only known the terrible avenging Christ of mediaeval Catholicism, and the pale vague Christ of the Humanists, just a little greater than Socrates; nor had he bestowed upon either a serious thought or a genuine feeling. This Christ was different–this Christ whom Agostino loved and trusted, to whose presence he was glad to go, and in whose Fathers house there were many mansions.

But-ever and anon, as these thoughts flitted through his mind, he was called back to the present by the horrible blackness of darkness, the stifling heat, the uneasy jolting of his narrow prison. Would this never end? Were they carrying him all round the city? Was he betrayed to certain death, and death in its most abhorrent form? No, not that. His trust in Theodore was unbounded. Still, he had leisure to ask himself the question many times, and to find an answer as best he could, before a halt and a parley with his bearers announced that the church was reached at last.

, Was ever light so sweet to human eyes as the faint and sickly glare of the tapers that burned upon the altar in that dim old church? Was ever face so beautiful as that of Theodore when–having wrenched off the frail ill-fitting coffin-lid with the strength of a giant–he stooped over his rescued friend, every feature beaming with triumph?

CHAPTER XV.

STRONGEB CHAINS BROKEN.

"To be wroth with one we love Doth work like madness on the brain."

HE rapture of recovered freedom was delicious, but it might be dangerous. Not long did Theodore allow Eaymond to indulge it. He took him to the sacristy, and furnished him with clothing, supplied by the friendly priest, and therefore likely to prove a safe and suitable disguise. Then he brought him to his own lodging, which was nigh at hand. His inclination had led him to Trastevere, a quarter of the city in which many of his brethren re sided; while his ample means enabled him to provide himself with handsome apartments in the Lungaretta, the best street of the locality. As they passed along, the August sun flashed up in glory, and Raymond grew faint and dizzy with the unaccustomed splendour. His friend supported his tottering footsteps, until at last they reached a quiet room, with blinds closely drawn, where Giulio stood waiting to welcome them, having divested himself of the hideous black cloak and hood of the becchino. Raymond grasped his hand, and poured out fervent thanks for his share in the rescue.

"Thank God, signor," was the answer. " I have but fulfilled the will of my master, and he has but fulfilled the will of God."

"That is more than I say for myself, good Giulio," said Theodore.

"You will say it one day, signor doctor," returned Giulio quietly, as he left the room.

Then, for the first time, Raymond tried to find words for his gratitude to Theodore.

"Truest of friends hast them been to me," he said.

"You would have done as much in my place," replied Theodore; "you, who are no son of Israel. As for us, our loves and our hates are alike intense, and they last from generation to generation."

"One word, dearest Theodore. How fares my mother?"

"She. has been ill; but the news of thy deliverance will be her best medicine. Fain would she have come hither to plead thy cause in person with the Pope; but my father withheld her, telling her it would not serve thee. Nor would it have done so."

"I will go to her. And the sooner I go the better. In all probability my escape will be discovered this morning, and search will be made for me. I shall endanger you."

"It is but too certain you must leave Eome, and that immediately. But not for Venice. The Pope is a Venetian, and the Signory, for a miracle, are but too complaisant to his Holiness at present. They have allowed him to get into his clutches your master, Pomponius Laetus, for whom you have all suffered more than he deserves."

"Say not that, Theodore."

"Well, perhaps I need not. Why should a man be a martyr for old-world habits, and uncertain speculations, and curious Latinity? Or for aught else, indeed?"

"Save for friendship," said Kaymond. "Or love."

"True; for love. But to return to your matters. The heat is fierce; you cannot travel until nightfall. Still, as you may be sought for in the city during the day, it is best we should agree upon some lonely spot–say in the Borghese Gardens–where I can find you to-night, and bring you what is necessary for your journey."

"But whither can I go, if not to Venice?"

"Back with me to Montpellier."

There followed a discussion of some length, and Eaymond, while he talked and listened, partook with his friend of a more hearty meal than he had enjoyed since his imprisonment. He was disposed to anticipate, with hope and pleasure, the long journey before him; and he had reasons of his own for wishing to visit Languedoc, which had ever been with him the land of romance and dreams.

"It is strange enough," he said, "that I am bound by a solemn promise to ga thither one day–and why not now? " " You never told me about that." " I told no one; that too was a promise, though meant, I suppose, only to bind my heedless youth. From thee, and now, I can have no secrets. One of my forefathers, a crusading knight, has bequeathed to our family a legend about a treasure buried in the garden of his ancestral home. My grandfather, on his death-bed, made me promise to go and seek for it one day. Should I succeed it will be doubly welcome, now that I am as bare of this worlds goods as when I came into it. Even my clothes and my books I can never hope to see again."

With the happy light-heartedness of youth he laughed at his own destitution, more than satisfied with the one priceless jewel he had won back–the pearl of freedom.

"Giulio, though an Italian by birth, has gone up and down in Languedoc for many a year, and knows every rood of the land. And you may trust him utterly. It were well therefore to take him into counsel. Have you any clear indication of the spot where this treasure is supposed to be?"

"Yes; an exact description, which I have always worn about my person, though I have not read it for years. In fact, it is in the Romance tongue, which I could not easily understand. Here it is."

He took from its place the little silken bag that contained his treasures; and as he drew out his reliquary out of it, the half circle of silver fell upon the table.

Then there swept over the face of Theo dore one of those swift, sudden changes possible only to the children of the fiery East. He touched the toy with a trembling finger, and said, in tones that scarcely seemed his own–

"Whence comes that, Count Eaymond?"

Eaymond was not looking up.

"Oh, that? "he answered with a blush and a smile, for in this happy hour his whole soul was flung open to the sunshine, and secret hopes and aspirations blossomed into instantaneous flower under the magic of its touch. " Dont you remember, long ago, when we were boys at the Academy of Venice, how we one day succoured a distressed damsel in the Piazza San Marco?"

"Allow me to correct you, Count Eaymond; you. were a boy, I was a man."

"That day I picked up this, and stored it as a relic; and then I sought once and again, with boyish admiration, a sight of the sweet face of her whose hand it had touched. But soon we were parted; I came hither, as thou knowest, to complete my studies."

"Was there no high-born Roman lady amongst the Orsini, the Savelh, the Colonna, the Rovere who were Count Raymonds daily associates, upon whom he could have fixed his wandering fancy?"

"Oh! I had wandering fancies enough; I blush to own it. Six times at least I imagined myself in love. Until she came–and then I knew the gold from the tinsel. For these things a man has no words. This only will I say, with Viola di Porcaro yesterdays dungeon would have been a Paradise; without her, or the hope of winning her, to-days freedom would be a dungeon."

"Count Raymond, I have heard your story. Now hear mine."

"My friend,–my friend,–what has happened?" cried Raymond, horror-stricken at the look in his companions face.

"Only what happens every day between Jew and Christian," said Theodore with intense bitterness. " Another edition of the old parable Nathan told David. Moreover, a little touch is added which rather heightens the effect. The poor man had just saved the rich mans life at some risk to himself."

"Dearest Theodore! " cried Raymond in great distress, as the truth broke at last upon his mind. " I never dreamed of this! How could I?"

"How could you not? Were you not aware that I ministered to her every need, and to those of her grandfather? That I was there every day?"

"You forget that I left Venice nearly a year before you did."

"I forget nothing." He rose, unlocked a strong box that lay upon a cabinet at one side of the room, and took out a half-ring of silver corresponding exactly with Bay-monds. "I too have kept my token since that day," he said, " though I cannot boast, like a love-sick boy, of wearing it next my heart."

The taunt was but a dash of spray flung up from the fount of bitterness that slumbers in the depths of every strong human heart.

"I never dreamed you had it," Eaymond said with truth.

"I think you might have dreamed–but let that pass," Theodore resumed in a gentler tone. " I have heard you–now hear me. As for you, you own you have had six fancies–this is the seventh. As for me, I have known since manhood dawned this one passion, this one hope–no other. To become worthy of Viola di Porcaro I have toiled, and striven, and endured. I have won successes in the schools, stooped to pick up honours my heart despised, turned my learning into gold and glory for her sake. But, you will tell me, I am a Jew–what chance has one of the accursed race against untainted blood, Christian faith? Not so fast, Count Raymond Chalcondyles. Eemember, she too belongs, by birth, to the ranks of the outlawed–her father died on the gibbet in the Castle of St. Angelo, and he died imshriven. Moreover, she is poor and friendless; her kinsfolk (curse them!) care for her but little, may force her, any day, to enter a convent. But were the distance between us ten times greater, I will try what courage, faith, patience, and the skill that is born of thought and experience can do to bridge it over. Thus have I sworn. Now, Count Raymond, are we to be friends or foes?"

Raymonds head drooped on his hands. The alternative was very bitter. On the one side, ingratitude to the friend who had just saved him from a fate worse than death–on the other, abandonment of his dearest earthly hopea. Which should he give up, Theodore or Viola? Still, the mans heart could find but one answer.

Once more he raised his head, and the two gazed steadfastly, each in the others face. Characters of race never seen before, at least by Raymond, had now become visible in Theodores–a look of resistance, fierce, determined, sullen, as of a creature brought to bay and fighting to the last–a look, not quite of hatred, but still the look of a man who could hate with unspeakable intensity. It was he who spoke first.

"Count Eaymond, I have loved you more than brother loves brother; yet, should you bar my way here, I tell you I will strike you from my path–if I can."

"And I," said Kaymond–for his spirit was kindling too–"I will refer my cause to her who alone has the right to decide between us."

"What! As you are? A hunted fugitive? But do what you please, I do not pretend to control your actions," returned Theodore, with the coldness that covers strong passion.

"But do not let us part in wrath," Raymond pleaded.

"There is no question of wrath. Only, I do not suppose the poor man in the parable regarded his wealthy neighbour with very lively affection."

Theodore feared. Raymond as a rival exceedingly; strange compound as he was of pride and humility, he greatly undervalued his own personal advantages, and thought the brilliant, beautiful young Greek must be well-nigh irresistible. Sorely tempted was he to hate him for it. The power to love implies a corresponding capability of jealousy, as strong light implies deep shadow. Moreover, the ancient prophetic doom of hia race rang in his ears, and sounded like a knell to his heart. " Thou shalt be only oppressed and spoiled evermore, and no man shall save thee. Thou shalt betroth a wife, and another man shall take her; thou shalt build a house, and thou shalt not dwell therein; thou shalt plant a vineyard, and shalt not gather the grapes thereof. Thy sons and-thy daughters shall be given unto another people, and thine eyes shall look, and fail with longing for them all the day long: and there shall be no might in thine hand." So long had he brooded, in the depths of his angry soul, upon oppression, violence, and wrong, that his eye could see nought else, whithersoever it turned, but the sombre hues to which it was accustomed. The natural interest which Viola, with all her kindred, had evinced in the fate of Raymond was now transformed into the evidence of a very different feeling. And Raymonds silence on the subject at their first meeting, which was no more singular than his own, became an evidence of deep and treacherous design.

"So it was for this I rescued you," he resumed at last. "Be it so. Try the power of your fair face, your soft eyes, your pleading voice–ay, even your misfortunes, against the sour-faced, world-hardened Jew physician, with his furred robe and gold-headed cane. Tell the signorina how you dreamed of her bright eyes in the dungeon of St. Angelo, while your rival lost his time dreaming of you and your rescue. To be sure you have at present no fortune to outweigh the certainty of a very comfortable establishment at Montpellier; but you have a buried treasure somewhere, if you can only find it."

"Not from any other in the whole world would I hear such words," said Eaymond. " And even from you I will hear no more of them. While we talk time passes. Every moment increases my danger, and yours, if I am found here. I have no longer the right to imperil you; and so, farewell. May God have you in His keeping, and may He show you my innocence towards you."

"God? "Theodore repeated, in a tone of bitter incredulity that revealed too clearly the real root of his want of faith in man. Ere the mocking echo of the word had died away Eaymond was gone past recall.

. The old cobbler who sat at the corner between the Lungaretta and the Piazza di Santa Maria paused in the song with which lie lightened his toil, to observe to his friend the fruitseller, "See that poor young priest vith the sad face hurrying up the street, keeping on the sunny side too, as if he were a dog or a foreigner. Per Bacco! he will have a sunstroke."

"He is going, no doubt, to some dying man. Stay him not."

"Ay, stay him not. I warrant me it is to some one who has been stabbed in a fray."

Then, with admirable consistency, the two friends together beset Raymond. "A bunch of grapes for a baiocco! Two pears for a mezzo-baiocco! "–" Mend your reverences shoes for a couple of baiocchi." While half-a-dozen idle bystanders chimed in, and began to whine out their petitions for charity " for the sake of God and the blessed Virgin."

Raymond, hearing the word "baiocco," a sound too familiar to ah l sojourners in Rome, mechanically thrust his hands into the pockets of his soutane, to perform what every Roman who had a pocket was taught to consider the first of Christain and social duties. Their absolute emptiness seemed to startle him; but he only shook his head, and walked rapidly on, pursued by a torrent of words which, it is to be feared, were not blessings; at least, the sound of "apoplexy" was distinctly audible more than once. He passed quickly through the Piazza, never halting until he reached the door of Santa Maria. Then, after a moments pause, he ascended the steps, and plunged out of the blazing sunlight into the darkness of the grand old church.

For an instant its antique legend flashed across his mind, as irrelevant thoughts are wont to do in hours of intense excitement. Here, it was said, had a fountain of oil sprung up miraculously on the same day that the oil of joy for the whole toiling suffering world had been poured forth in the birth, far away, of the Babe of Bethlehem. With slackened pace he ascended the seven steps that led to the transept, and then stood looking at the worn inscription in the pavement, "Fons olei," which indicated the site of the alleged miracle. But no marvel of the distant past could hold him long from thoughts of the nearer past of his own brief history, when he used to haunt that church for a glimpse of Viola. He felt as though it would still the tumult within him to breathe a prayer where she had prayed so often.

" May you have an apoplexy! "still the favourite imprecation of the Eoman beggar if refused an alms. Its sting lies in the idea that the sufferer would be unable to receive the last rites of the Church.

At an altar near that of St. Philip and St. James a priest was doing something, and a few market-women and contadini were kneeling around muttering prayers. Raymond went forward and knelt amongst them, and from his confused troubled spirit, darkened though it was with a heavy cloud of ignorance, there arose a murmur, like the lisping of a child, to One great and good, who, as he dimly hoped, would hear and help him.

As he rose his eye sought out a well-known object, one of the curious antique columns that supported the church, conspicuous amongst the others for its size and for the representations of heathen deities that adorned its Ionic capital. Behind this pillar, as he well knew, had been interred, not inappropriately, the remains of the brave old Roman, Stefano Porcaro, though even the hand of affection had not dared to mark the plain slab that covered them, save with a cross, two letters, and a date. And now, beside that grave, two persons were standing, apparently in earnest conversation–Viola di Porcaro herself, and Theodores servant G-iulio.

Viola wore, as usual, her dress of deep mourning; but her sweet face shone with an animation he had never seen in it before. The fawn-eyed, frightened child of the Piazza San Marco was a woman now–a grave, thoughtful woman, with a brow shadowed evermore by the reflection of a great sorrow. She looked like one whose heart

"Sat silent thro the noise And concourse of the street."

These are now removed.

Very beautiful indeed she was, but not with the rich beauty of the Roman maid, ripened by the kiss of southern suns. Viola was a flower that had grown in the shade–she had the delicacy, the grace, the fragrance of her namesake. Raymond stood and gazed; indemnifying himself by that gaze for the lonely months that had been–the lonely years that were to be, if his foreboding heart spoke true.

And there, all the time, stood the grave, mysterious scholar whom Theodore called his servant; no doubt delivering messages from him, and pleading his cause. It was a pity that Raymonds delicate sense of honour kept him just outside earshot, or he might have been undeceived. The words that had such power to bring the light to Violas eye and the colour to her cheek were not those of earthly hope or love. But this Raymond could not guess. As he watched and waited the fire burned in his heart. If Theodore all this time had been working for himself, then his hands were

"Baymond and Viola, hand clasped in hand."

unbound, he might do the same. He was a hunted fugitive–yesterday a prisoner, to-morrow an exile–he had suffered long and terribly. Was not the poor man free to ask an alms, the traveller free to beg a God speed" to help him on his way? And yet, poor as he was, it might be that fortune had left him somewhat to offer that Viola di Porcaro might not quite disdain. Had he not a true heart, a princely name, a buried treasure?

Meanwhile Giulio bowed respectfully, and moved away. As he reached the door, a con-tadina, leading a child by the hand, dipped her finger in the vessel of holy water, crossed herself on the forehead, and did the same to the little one; then she stepped courteously aside to allow the stranger to perform the pious ceremony. This, however, Giulio chose to decline, but that he might do so with less observation, he turned back for a moment into the church, and thus it happened that he saw Raymond and Viola standing together, hand clasped in hand.

CHAPTER XVI.

GIULIO.

"The dumb, dread people that sat,
All night without screen for the night,
All day without food for the day,

They shall not give their harvest away,
They shall eat of its fruit and wax fat;
They shall see the desire of their sight.
Tho the way of the seasons be steep,
They shall climb it with face to the light,
Put in the sickle and reap."

JNE of the grandest chapters in all history has yet to be written adequately–the epic of the long conflict between humanity and Rome. Should some transcendant poet-historian arise, joining the heart of fire to comprehend high impulses and heroic issues with the hand of patient industry to piece together confused and fragmentary details, he would have to begin far back in the dim twilight of modern society, with–

"The world-wide throes
That went to make the Popedom–the despair
Of free men, brave men, good men."

But where he would have to end, God only knoweth, who knoweth all things.

Funeral piles, fed with living bodies, flash out here and there, all through the gloomy darkness of mediaeval times. Now and again some strange, awful tragedy arrests our gaze and freezes our blood with horror; some tale, like Dolcinos, of cruel oppression provoking wild resistance to be crushed at last with cruelty yet more appalling. Then, there is the great, dark blood-stain, never more to be effaced, which blotted out for ever the glory and the prosperity of the fair land of the troubadours. There is the long martyr-story of the simple and harmless race who dwelt in Alpine valleys. But besides the Albigenses of Languedoc, the Waldenses of Piedmont and their colonies, there are a few well-known names familiar to every ear–such as Peter Waldo, John Wickliffe, John Huss, Jerome of Prague, the lord of Cobham; samples of many more, which are written only in the book of Gods remembrance.

The horrible but heroic story may be read in Milmans "History of Latin Christianity," vol. vii. pp. 359-367. It seems to have fascinated the poet soul of Kingsley. See the short poems "Margaret to Dolcmo," " Dolcino to Margaret," and a very striking passage in " Two Years Ago."

Yet the historian of Protestantism should be on his guard against a very natural, but very serious mistake. It does not follow that every foe of Bome was a friend of truth, of freedom, of Christ. It must be remembered, on the one hand, that Rome was the representative of spiritual law and of social order, and therefore most of those to whom law and order were abhorrent found themselves in the ranks of her enemies; on the other, that the very darkness of the times engendered hideous forms of moral and mental corruption, so that Eomes sole responsibility, with regard to some sects of the Middle Ages, seems to lie in this, that they could not have existed at all had she not left the surrounding community in a depth of ignorance and depravity that made all horrible delusions possible and contagious. Without doubt Eome has sent many a man to the stake who, at least, fully deserved the gibbet.

Therefore it is impossible for mortal eye wholly to penetrate the darkness that overhangs this part of the great battle-field between truth and error. Eome herself has been the historian of her enemies; and she has enveloped them all in one black sulphureous smoke of undistinguishing anathemas. Here and there, through the smoke, we may catch the gleam of a robe so white that malice itself cannot tarnish its pure lustre; for instance, the Waldenses of Piedmont and the Poor Men of Lyons may be considered above reproach, their enemies themselves being judges. But, besides these, a vast multitude. of indistinct and shadowy forms throng and press around us; and sometimes we dimly recognise the mystic, the Manichsean, the profligate materialist, side by side with the devout believer, whose only heresy was the rejection of an absurd and degrading superstition.

Unworthy indeed were the Protestant who, for controversial purposes, should assume aught respecting these enemies of Eome beyond what may be proved, or reasonably inferred, from recorded facts. For it is the very life and essence of Protestantism to set truth before all else; to believe nothing because it is convenient, or comfortable, or interesting, or aesthetic, or even edifying–unless it be true. That God is light, and that in Him is no darkness at all; that God is truth, and that no He is of the truth, is the keynote of Protestantism. Therefore, for a Protestant to take falsehood as his weapon, and to stab Eome with a lie, would be both a blunder and a baseness.

No time was more disastrous for the enemies of Rome than the second half of the fifteenth century, though it proved eventually only the dark hour before the dawning of the day. It seemed almost as if all protesting voices were to be silenced at last. The fierce religious wars of Bohemia were dying out, and even there the dominant party amongst the Hussites, the Calixtines, could not properly be styled sectaries, as they only differed from Rome upon a point of ceremonial, and were sincerely anxious for the recognition of the Church. It is true that then, as ever, the Waldenses of the Alps maintained their testimony; and the same was done in Bohemia by a few poor oppressed communities of United Brethren. Besides these, and in other countries, isolated witnesses for the faith once delivered to the saints were never wholly wanting.

They gave the cup to the laity, but held all other doctrines and ceremonies of the Bomish Church. From the-Taborites, or more advanced Hussite party, sprang the truly Evangelical Church of the " United Brethren."

For a clear and interesting account of the religious struggles in Bohemia during this century see " The Ee-fonners before the Keformation," bye. de Bonnechose.

Such a witness was the wandering scholar who, for reasons of his own, had consented for a time to act as servant to Dr. Theodore Benedetto. Giulio was by birth an Italian, and he had been early trained in the practice of a curious and delicate handicraft, which was almost a fine art. Thus faculties naturally keen were developed and educated; but he was thoughtful and speculative as well as quick and dexterous, and as he watched beside the furnace where his crystal vases were being annealed to the point of absolute perfection, he had time to ponder many things in heaven and earth. He grew dissatisfied, first with the parish priest to whom he applied for the solution of some of his difficulties, then with priests, monks, and friars in general, lastly with the whole Church system. By night and by day his dreams were of reform, possible and impossible. Already had his soul felt the magnetic touch of spiritual aspiration, but there were many vibrations of the needle before it pointed to the pole of Truth and settled there, to move no more for ever. There was a time when he seemed likely to become the founder of a new religious order; and indeed Eome has cursed many whom, under conditions slightly altered, she would have canonized, and canonized some whom she might easily have cursed. Giulios indignation against the prevailing Mariolatry decided his fate. In an ebullition of ill-regulated zeal he one day destroyed an image of the Virgin which was an object of especial reverence to the workmen of his craft. He had to flee from their vengeance for his life, although afterwards their esprit de corps led them secretly to repair the image and to hush up the scandal amongst themselves.

He made his way to the south of France, where the art he was able to practise and to teach secured him the means of comfortable subsistence. It would even have raised him to honour and affluence could he have found rest for the sole of his foot. But he was still in search of a faith, and his unquiet heart made him a wanderer up and down the land. Blood and fire had extinguished almost every trace of the Albi-genses, but here and there a few hidden sparks of the old life smouldered amongst the ashes. Wherever Giulio perceived a disposition to resist the tyranny of the Church and the exactions of the priesthood, he fouowed up the scent carefully and patiently, though in most cases with no result except disappointment. Once, however, he was fortunate enough to meet an intelligent and enlightened old man, who put into his hand the celebrated " Nobla Leyeon " of the Waldenses. It came upon his thirsting soul like rain from heaven. Its brief, calm words, simple with the unadorned simplicity of Scripture narrative and exhortation, showed him what he longed to know, how to refuse the evil and to choose the good in the creed of his childhood. With this help, and that of such fragments of Holy Scripture as he could gather out of missals and breviaries, he shaped his faith. A whole Bible he had never seen; but he afterwards visited a community of United Brethren in Bohemia, and he found with them the Gospel and the Eevelation of St. John, and the Epistle of St. Paul to the Bomans, which they had obtained from the Waldenses in the Eomance dialect, although they had translated them into German for their own use. Giulio copied them for himself, and profited greatly by the occupation.

He was now as one who had dwelt all his life amidst the obscure alleys of a city, and who yields, perhaps reluctantly, to those who persuade him to go forth and see green fields and budding flowers. The loss of old surroundings and associations, which he had feared so greatly, was swallowed up in the sense of a gain absolutely immeasurable;–for a narrow strip of blue, the whole vault of azure; for crowded streets and dusky lanes, the free campaign and the boundless, limitless ocean. At last his soul found freedom and peace. No longer was there any veil between him and God his Father, Christ his Eedeemer, the Divine Spirit his Sanctifier.

The impulse to teach was as strong upon him now as the desire to learn had been before. He went to and fro through the earth, seeking out the sorrowful, the lonely, the doubting, to bring them the message of the love of God, and the way of access to Him which is open evermore through Christ. Of course his path was one of continual peril, as that of the apostle who " died daily;" for the message he bore had in it the seed of Eomes downfall, even if his own hostility to the dominant Church had not been like " the ointment of his right hand," that "bewrayed itself" continually.

But this very hostility gave him a powerful friend in Dr. Theodore, who made his acquaintance first as a patient, and then was attracted by his shrewdness and insight as well as by the courage with which he avowed his opinions. Giulio was anxious, for many reasons, to revisit his native land, and Theodore offered to take him thither if he would assume for the time the position and the duties of his confidential servant. The arrangement succeeded admirably. Giulio proved abundantly useful to his temporary master, and the relation between them became every day more intimate. As they laboured together for the deliverance of Raymond, Theodore could not sufficiently admire the courage, the tact, and the fertility of resource which Giulio had learned in half a lifetimes conflict with persecution. Giulio entered the capital of Christendom full of the hope of finding secret brethren there, as he had done already in other cities. He was disappointed; the nobles seemed abandoned to violence, luxury, and profligacy, while the common people were sunk in sloth and venality. True sons of the slaves of Caligula and Tiberius, who used to raise the cry " Panem et circenses," love of gain and love of pleasure seemed the only passions they were capable of cherishing. Giulios brightest hours in Rome–except perhaps those spent in penning the letter that soothed the deathbed of Campano–were the hours in which he sought to lighten the dark cloud that overhung the soul of Viola di Porcaro. It was something to make her understand that to die, as her father died, " unhouseld, disappointed, unaneld," was not necessarily to die unrepentant and forsaken of God; it was more to make her see that she herself was not alone in the world, a mere burden upon the cold good-will of relatives who cared not for her–since she too had a Father in heaven.

On the eventful day of which we are tracing the history, Giulio returned at once from the church to the lodging of his patron, thinking that now Count Raymond had gone forth (as he doubted not, with Theodores, full concurrence), Theodore would probably wish to take counsel with him.

He was struck at once by a change in the appearance of his patron. Theodore looked an older and a sadder man–and, if all must be said, a worse man too–than he had done that morning. His dark eyes burned with a dull and sullen glare, and there was a shadow on his brow, as though he were brooding over some bitter wrong.

"So, Signor Doctor, Count Kaymond has gone. forth, and in daylight. Is that prudent? " said Giulio.

"How do you know? " asked Theodore sharply.

"I met him just now in the church yonder. I left him there, holding converse with the Signorina Viola di Porcaro, at her fathers grave."

The words were fuel to the fire of Theodores wrath. " Ay? Then he has gone straight from my presence to hers! And it was for this I saved him, the traitor!"

Master, dear master, what is the matter?" asked Giulio in great surprise. Partly from Theodores reserve of character, partly from the singular want of observation in such matters sometimes shown by men otherwise exceedingly shrewd, he had no idea of his patrons feelings towards Viola.

Theodore turned on him a look half-indignant, half-imploring. " Go, Giulio," he said; " go from my presence while yet I can restrain myself. Go, or I shall say that which will ring in your ears for ever. I gave my substance, my time, my thought, ay, and freely would I have given my life, to save that boy from his doom, and now–would to God I had let him rot in the dungeon of St. Angelo!"

"Master, you are giving place to the devil," said Giulio with sorrowful sternness, drawing nearer and laying his hand on his arm.

"Curse your old-world superstitions! " cried Theodore, roughly shaking off his grasp. " Go! I would be alone."

"I obey. But, Signor Doctor, the young Count, however he may have offended you, is friendless, penniless, and in great peril. Let me try to find him."

"No; let the Porcari look to him, if they will. Go!"

Giulio obeyed, and for a perplexed and anxious hour listened to Theodores agitated footsteps, as he paced up and down above his head.

Then he was summoned once more to his presence. Theodore had regained the outward composure and dignity of bearing he so seldom allowed himself to lose; but he looked pale and stern. " Have you completed your business here? " he asked quietly, and even courteously.

"Yes, Signor Doctor. There is, indeed, but little I can do. There seems no fuel here to be taken hold of by the sacred fire. Mens hearts are eaten out by sloth and sin and selfishness; there is no earnestness even in error. But Grod can do all things," he concluded with a sigh. "Pack up, then, for we leave this tomorrow at daybreak. Best away from Rome now, at all events; the heat is stifling."

"And whither next, Signor Doctor?"

"To Venice."

A flash of pleasure lit up Giulios grave features as he responded briefly, "I am glad! " In all the world, Venice was the place whither he most desired to go.

Meanwhile, the stern admonition he had addressed to his patron was becoming every moment more sadly true. Theodore was giving himself tip to the power of the spirit of evil, the " Divider," the " Accuser." Under that malignant spell, the strong love of which his soul was capable was changing into hatred. He could be tender, self-sacrificing, faithful–he could have been all this even unto death–but there are stronger things than death. Treason loosens all bonds. " No friendship," he assured himself, "covild have endured this strain and lived. No; not that of my namesake and ancestor, though his love for David was wonderful. Sauls javelin was easily borne: had David aimed his at him in the dark, I wonder what would have become of the oath of God that was between them.–Ah, yes; I remember! No doubt I spoke of Viola, hinted my hopes, in that last letter I wrote to him from Montpellier. He kept his secret well that night we met–that night of his arrest. Nigh six months of my life since then worse than lost, toiling and striving for him. No; on second thoughts I cannot go to Venice, to meet my fathers eye, and to tell him all. My dear father! After all, no friend so true as a good father. Between the young and the old there is a great gulf fixed; yet the old care for the young as the young never care for each other, stedfastly and selflessly. Still, no–not now to Venice. His mother, too, is there. I will send Giulio with letters and messages; that will please him, since he evidently desires to go on his own account. But as for me, I will take another way."

All this passed through the mind of Theodore, not in the form of soliloquy–his nature was too strong and direct for that–but as thought fused red-hot in the fire of passion. Wroth with Raymond as he was, "even unto death," he never dreamed of avenging himself by any overt act. All he would do was to stand aside and leave him alone. But if that meant, as most likely it did mean, leaving him to perish, "His blood be upon his own head," said Theodore Benedetto.

Half an hour afterwards, Giulio opened the door and ushered in a gentleman rather showily attired, and with a kind of bravado in his look and manner which concealed, not very successfully, no small amount of anxiety and uneasiness. " II Signor Gae-tano Benedetto," he said; and Theodore, much surprised, rose up to welcome his eldest brother.

CHAPTER XVII.

FAREWELLS.

"Als ich Abschied uahm, als ich Abschied nahm
Waren Kisten und Kasten schwer;
Als ich wieder kam, als ich wieder kam,
War alles leer."

HAYMOND left the church of Santa Maria in Trastevere with a strange lightness of heart. He knew that he was a forlorn and hunted fugitive, with nowhere to lay his head, and not a coin in his pocket wherewith to purchase the simplest necessaries of life; and he feared that he had alienated for ever the friend who had been to him as a brother. And yet he could have sung aloud for very joy and gladness of heart. He was free, the whole world was before him, and Viola di Porcaro had not denied that she loved him. He could afford to think of Theodore with tender, remorseful pity. Fate had been very hard on him–very; and well and patiently would Kaymond seek in the. after years to recompense his generous kindness, and to win back his love.

But in the meantime the August sun was blazing down upon his head, and he must find shelter somewhere. Whither could he bend his steps? He would find no welcome, even in a wine-shop, without a baiocco to pay for a draught of wine. Should he have recourse to Cardinal Bessarion, in former days a munificent patron of the Humanists, and even now, in their time of persecution, their steady, though cautious friend? Unfortunately for him the good cardinal was " in villegiatura," having wisely exchanged the stifling heat and fever-laden atmosphere of the city for the refreshing breezes of the Albanian hills.

Another resource occurred to him. Be- tween the Humanists and the printers there existed a close friendship and alliance. Both belonged to the new age that was dawning on the world, both were labourers in the same cause, the cause of intellectual light and liberty. Two liberal-minded Germans, Conrad Sweynheim and Arnold Manetz, had lately established a printing press in Eome under the friendly patronage of the Bishop of Aleria, who had been one of the pupils of the excellent Vittorino de la Feltre. Kay-mond thought of taking up, for a time, the compositors stick, and finding at once daily bread and effectual concealment in the " chapel," or workshop, of the Palazzo Mas-sario.

But the risk was too great. What if the fiery Pope should discover his retreat, and wreak his vengeance on the harmless printers, scattering their type, shutting up their workshop, and perhaps destroying their priceless MSS.? Eaymond shuddered at the thought, and decided that nothing should tempt him so to endanger them, and the great cause they and he alike represented.

While pondering thus he crossed the Ponte Sisto, and finding himself among the narrow crowded streets on the other bank of the Tiber, he walked aimlessly onwards. But he soon began to feel weak and weary, for the unaccustomed exercise told quickly upon limbs long confined to a prison cell. Having wandered as far as the Palazzo Cenci, he sat down to rest and to ponder his situation under the high narrow archway of that ill-fated mansion, whose gloomy and sinister aspect already seemed to forebode the dark tragedy of which it was one day to be the theatre. Here, in the shade, the drowsy spirit of the Roman noontide stole over him, and he was about to indulge in a brief siesta, when he fortunately remembered that under his present circumstances nothing could possibly be more dangerous, and, rousing himself with a strong effort, he shook off the inclination to slumber. Now, when all Rome was asleep, must he be awake and stirring; too soon would the shops be unclosed and the silent streets once more full of life and business.

A great longing came over him to revisit the garden on the Quirinal, where he had spent so many happy hours, listening to the discourses of Pomponius or holding converse with him and his friends. So he stepped silently and slowly through the streets and squares of the sleeping city–sleeping more profoundly now than in the noon of night–scarce a sound breaking on his ear, save the musical trickle and murmur of Romes many fountains. Here and there a beggar, dozing in the shade, turned and looked up, murmuring a drowsy prayer for baiocchi, but found it too much trouble even to curse him for refusing, and turned over again to finish his siesta. His own footsteps grew feeble and listless long before his goal was reached. With tottering feet he passed along the familiar Via Cornelia, gazed with a mournful sigh at the Lecture Hall–so dearly loved in other days–and almost as sadly at the beautiful villa which his friend Platina had scarcely completed when he was forced to exchange it for a gloomy cell in the Castle of St. Angelo. He was glad to find himself at last beneath the olives and evergreen oaks of his masters garden. The trees were unchanged, but all else had run riot, or bore the marks of confusion and decay. The borders of box, once so quaint and. square-cut, trimmed as they were by the masters own hand after the antique pattern, now grew freely as their nature prompted. The succulent cabbages, broccoli, and lettuces which had been the masters pride as much as that of Diocletian, had fallen a prey to the petty pilferers of the neighbourhood, and only foul, decaying refuse was left to taint the air. But in compensation luscious roses shed their leaves and their perfumes unheeded, and all varieties of bright southern summer flowers threw themselves about in a wild tangle of colour and sweetness, interlacing their stems and mingling their blossoms.

The heart of Baymond grew sad over the desolation. He laid himself down under an olive-tree, and the motifnful thoughts that oppressed him found relief in tears. The masters school seemed to him like the masters garden. Where was now the band of noble youths that used to cluster around him beneath the shadow of those trees, or within the walls of that Lecture Hall, so near at hand? One was in his grave, a martyr to his faithful love for him; the rest were captives, fugitives,–or at best they were cowed, silent, and dismayed. The wind of destruction had swept over all.

But there are some things that are indestructible. Had the storm of persecution scattered a congregation of primitive Christians on that very hill, broken up a synagogue in the Trastevere, dispersed a conventicle of sectaries like Giulio in some fair Provencal valley, yet all these, or what they represented, would have risen undecayed from the ashes of their ruin. Was the Koman Academy like these? Did Pomponius Laetus and

Ms disciples represent phases of thought and feeling that were passing, or principles that were permanent? Could these dry bones live again? The answer Raymonds heart foreboded was a mournful negative, and he was partly, though not wholly, in the right. In these ardent students the passion of the Age for antiquity, its thirst for the inspiration to be caught from the mighty spirits of old, found expression, and so far they fulfilled a need and accomplished a mission. But though they belonged to the new world–the world of modern thought and feeling–they were not great enough to conquer and to keep a place amongst its monarchs and rulers. Like other schools of the Renaissance, theirs had in it the seed of corruption in the fatal severance between intellectual and spiritual light, between knowledge and holiness. God was not in all their thoughts; and therefore when they themselves were taken away " their thoughts perished." Not however that the work of Pomponius Laetus was over at this time. In after days he was permitted to resume his teaching, and the Roman Academy flourished once more under his auspices. But although his labours and those of his friends and disciples– whose names now sound but faintly through the trumpet of fame–no doubt form part of the great intellectual heritage into which we have entered unconsciously, they only live, like the plants of his own garden, transmuted into the nourishment of other forms of life, not like the stately cedars that shelter a hundred generations beneath their spreading branches. Few care anything now for Pomponius Laetus and the Humanists of the Roman Academy. But even a temporary return of pros perity was beyond the anticipation of Eaymond. A chill and saddening sense of failure stole over his heart. The masters want of steadfastness to his principles had been a cruel blow to him. It seemed as if Pomponius could not bear, for the sake of his own honour, what others had borne so heroically for him. The modern representative of Brutus and Eegulus was on his knees at the feet of the Pope.

The death of Paul II. put an end to the persecution. His successor, Sixtus IV., allowed Pomponius Laetus to resume his lectures, which were continued with great success until almost the end of the century. He died in 1498. Sixtus made Platina curator of the Vatican library, and he became the historian of the Popes. He avenged himself, not unnaturally, by a spiteful portrait of Paul II.

All is well, though a standard-bearer fall, if the soldiers can raise their eyes to the kings own pennon, still waving proudly in the thickest of the fight. Eaymond had not this consolation. His soul owned allegiance to no master greater than Pomponius, and when his faith in him was shattered, it seemed as though the foundations of his intellectual life were giving way.

But the life, even of the body, is worth preserving–at least in this fair world, and with those left who love us and whom we love. Therefore Eaymond rose at last, and having found amongst the refuse a few lettuces still unspoiled, washed them at the spring, and appeased his hunger with this very primitive fare.

The noonday heat was now beginning to abate, and a fresh breeze was springing up. Eaymond looked at the distant hills, flecked with white and silvery clouds, and his soul longed for the rest and shelter they seemed to promise. Somewhere over there was the ancestral home of Campano, and had he not the last messages of his friend to deliver? Would not his kindred give him a welcome and a refuge? He did not doubt it. "And on the way," he said, " any contadino will share his hut with me."

CHAPTBE XVIII.

Theodores Trial.

"The champaign, with its endless fleece
Of feathery grasses everywhere!
Silence and passion, joy and peace,
An everlasting wash of air–
Eomes ghost since her decease."

SHEODOEE soon learned that his luckless half-brother had come to him as to a rock of safety in the midst of a sea of troubles. It was the old story of the prodigal son in its modern version: debt incurred recklessly and concealed with contemptible moral cowardice, the concealment doubling the evil, until at last a point was reached threatening absolute ruin, aggravated by terrible and deserved disgrace.

"But why did you not confide in our father, the most generous as well as the most righteous of men? " Theodore asked reproachfully.

Gaetano replied by pouring out a long, passionate, incoherent story ofdistrust and, disunion sown between him and his father by the arts of his brother Antonio. Theodore made large allowances for prejudice and exaggeration; yet, on the whole, he believed there was some truth in the representations of Gaetano. Since his boyhood he had recognized Antonio as one of those persons who, placed between any two others, invariably sunder them.

Gaetano pleaded earnestly with Theodore to return with him to Venice, help him to confess all to his father, and try to make peace between them. Should he refuse, he threatened to enlist immediately in a company of condottieri, and seek death on the battle-field. This was not to be thought of, both for their fathers sake, and on account of sundry young and helpless lives unhappily dependent upon the thoughtless prodigal. Therefore Theodore, with whom, as with most of his race, the bonds of family affection and sympathy were very strong, eventually yielded, and promised to accompany his brother.

They started at daybreak two days afterwards. During the noontide heat they stopped to rest at a desolate little wayside osteria. The place was silent and dreary. No contadini lounged on the stone bench before the door eating black bread and goats-milk cheese, and drinking the landlords sour wine; no passing wine-cart made the air musical with the merry tinkle of its bells; only the landlord himself, withered, yellow, and sickly, came out to take their horses, and to offer them the shelter of his roof–he had little else to offer.

Theodore had engaged half-a-dozen stout, well-armed serving men as an escort, for the roads were infested with banditti; and the party had brought provisions with them, Ina, of which they were now glad to avail themselves. After a frugal meal the travellers wrapped their cloaks around them, and stretched themselves on the ground, to enjoy a siesta.

But Theodore could not sleep. Many things made him restless. He reproached himself with having, after all, left Rome without seeking an explanation with Viola. Bitterly did he curse his own haughty reserve, which, as he now felt, had in all probability ruined his hopes for ever. His mind was full of Viola; he could turn it to no other subject, not even to the business that was bringing him to Venice. Slumber was impossible, and the effort to remain quiet became every moment more insupportable. At last he rose noiselessly, and, without awakening any of his companions, left the osteria.

He stood for some time looking over the silent landscape. The mournful beauty of the Campagna appealed powerfully to his heart. In the distance his eye rested upon the ruins of the grand old Eoman Aqueduct, with its miles of arches. Nearer, a wide grassy plain, broken here and there into mounds and hillocks, stretched out before him. Amid the green, patches of scarlet poppies and other bright summer flowers bloomed unheeded; or heaps of tumbled stones, half overgrown with vegetation, told that human life had once throbbed with full pulses over the scene which was now desolate, forsaken, and echoless. No sound, no cry of beast or bird, not so much as the chirp of a cicala, broke the stillness. The noontide heat had driven into hiding even the " lizards green and rare " that haunted the mouldering stones, and the " sad aziola," whose note suits her home so well. Far away, looking purple under the cloudless azure of the Italian sky, gleamed the Sabine hills.

Close at hand a ruined doorway and part of a wall showed where once had stood a Roman villa. It offered Theodore shelter from the sun, and perhaps the chance of finding a few rare flowers, about which he was anxious, as a keen student of nature. He reached it, gathered and examined the flowers, and then sat down in the shade to rest. It occurred to him that he had never opened a packet of letters received just before leaving Eome. He drew it out of the pocket of his doublet, untied the silk that bound it, and broke the seal. The first thing that met his eye was a letter of his own to Eaymond, the last written from Montpellier, which his agent there had returned to him, not finding the expected opportunity of forwarding it. Such mischances were common enough, and Theodore put by the letter without even reflecting that it cleared Eaymond of part of the blame attaching to him; since only in that letter, if at all, had he mentioned the name of Viola. Then came a communication from a friend and pupil at Montpellier; full of such items of news as those who seek the peace of the city where they sojourn like to receive during a temporary absence. The most noteworthy event recorded was the death of the Greek professor, a man of considerable talents, but of strong passions and irregular life.

Whilst he read, Theodore became aware of a deeper shadow thrown across his page, and, looking up, saw a shepherd of the Campagna standing before him. There was no mistaking the short jacket of undressed sheeps wool, the faded red waistcoat, the shaggy goat-skin trousers, even without the yellow gourd of water by his side, the long pole in his hand, and the sheep-dog at his heels.

Apparently the shepherd was in as little doubt about the calling of the doctor, who, though the heat had caused him to discard his robe, still carried his gold-headed cane, and was now making use of it to repel the rude advances of the shepherds dog.

"Scusi, Signor Doctor, scusi," said the dogs owner. " Down, Caesar, down! Dont you know a Signor Eccellenza when you see him? Eh, you brute? "

"He thinks I have some food about me," said Theodore. Then, raising his eyes from the dog to the shepherd, he observed his countenance, which was yellow, ghastly, and wrinkled. With a sentiment of compassion and an instinct of his calling, he took a broad silver coin from his purse. " Spend that on mutton collops or capon broth," he said, " and eschew sour wine and unsound fruit, if you wish to live, my friend. Why, in the name of Saint–whatsoever saint presides over common sense–dont you take your flock up to the mountains?"

The contadino thanked him profusely, invoked all the saints, and explained that he never went to the mountains–not he; the padrone did not wish it, for the flocka throve better on the rich grasses of the plain. Then he began again, "Scusi, Signor Doctor, scusi."

"Well, my man, what more do you want of me? Medicine?"

"Not for myself, oh no 1 I am not ill," said the poor fellow, though, as he spoke, his teeth were chattering with ague. " But, oh, Signor Doctor!–scasi."

"Well?"

"Over yonder, in my capanno, lies a stranger very ill–dying! A priest too, signor. Come to him, Signor Doctor, for the love of God and the saints!"

"It is the fever, of course. Those who breathe poison must expect the consequences," said Theodore. " And in these cases medicine can do but little. Still, since you ask it, I will just look at him; but I must first tell my friends at the osteria."

He did so; took with him some specifics with which he was always provided, and resigned himself to the guidance of the kind-hearted shepherd.

He could not help wondering, as he passed along, why a scene so fair and bright should be the lair of the pestilence " that walketh in darkness." Practical as ever, he pondered the question with a view to finding a solution and a remedy–but in Small thatched hut.

vain; the sad mystery of the malaria has been doomed to baffle investigation for many a long year after Theodore Benedetto slept with his fathers.

At last they reached the capanno, a rude hut of thick matted straw and sticks, very narrow, and not high enough for a man to stand upright. Fortunately a solitary oak stood near, and Theodore begged the shepherd, for the present, to seek its shade, as the hut, really too small for one, would be intolerable for three.

He passed in, stooping low. The sick man lay upon a heap of straw covered with a blanket. He seemed insensible, or at least unconscious of the approach of a stranger. Theodore took the burning hand in his, preparatory to a diagnosis of the case. As for this purpose he moved to his side, ceasing to block up the doorway with his own form, he saw clearly, for the first time, the face of the sufferer. It was the face of Raymond Chalcondyles.

The impulse of the moment was to give the contadino some money and some medicine, and to depart at once, before Raymond could recognize him. Theodore was not cruel, so at least he told himself; he would do what humanity demanded, even for his enemy. Raymond was his enemy. Not that now his wrath burned fiercely against him like fire; it rather resembled frost, the frost of an Arctic winter–bands of iron, " cold, strong, passionless," clasped about his heart.

. If thus abandoned Raymond would die. That was almost certain. His death would not lie at his door. What had induced him to wander into this haunt of fever? He must take the consequences of his own imprudence. Raymond would die; while as for himself, he would pursue his journey to Venice, complete his business there, and return to Rome to woo and win Viola di Porcaro. There would be no obstacle now, and nothing else in the world seemed worth anything to him that hour.

Raymond would die. He turned away from him; he would not look on his face again, lest his heart should relent, and the old love return. No danger of that–not now; his heart seemed dead within him. In fact, he was not thinking of Raymond at all; only of himself, and of the consequences to himself of his own actions.

"Theodore Benedetto, you are doing the deed of a villain! " Whence came the voice? Were the words spoken by him, or were they spoken to him by another? He never knew; and yet they sounded in his ears with terrible distinctness. It flashed upon his mind with irresistible force that so to leave Baymond–his friend or his enemy, whichever he pleased to call him–would be unworthy, base, vile. To stay with him, to watch by him, to win him back to life–this was the thing he ought to do.

Ought ? What did that mean? What word, "quick and powerful and sharper than any two-edged sword," reached and smote the very depths of his heart, telling him that the one course was right and the other wrong–and that between moral right and wrong there was a distance infinite as between heaven and hell? Theodore knew that if he left that shed, leaving Eaymond to his death, he himself would be lost. He would be a lost soul;–not indeed condemned in the future world to what he traditionally called Gehenna, and in which he now no longer believed, but lost, now evermore and for evermore, to truth and right, to justice and nobleness.

He shrank appalled from the gulf of moral degradation that opened before him. "No," he cried, "I will not be such a wretch as that. How could I dare to woo Viola di Porcaro? It would not be the old Theodore Benedetto who should offer her his heart, but a ghoul, who had slain him and taken possession of his body."

Yet how embrace the other alternative–serve Eaymond day and night like a brother, breathing for his sake this poisoned atmosphere, and using all his skill and science to win him back to life–for Viola? It seemed impossible–and yet it seemed inevitable. Almost in the same breath he said, "I cannot" and "I must." At last he threw himself on his knees beside the couch. " God of my fathers, Jehovah! " he cried, "Thou hast so made me that I know right from wrong. Thou hast written with Thy finger on my heart that right is high as heaven and wrong deep as the abyss of hell. But I am weak. I see the right, but I cannot love it. Help me at least to do it."

Eaymond turned, and moaned feebly, "Water, water! " Theodore rose, found a gourd with some water in it, and put it to his lips. Then he felt his pulse, prepared and administered some of the medicine he had brought, arranged his rude couch as comfortably as he could, and contrived to admit sufficient air, and yet to screen him from the light. Now he no longer debated with himself what course he should pursue. He felt as one who had no choice of his own, but was simply obeying orders.

But how could he plead Gaetanos cause with his father if he remained here with Baymond? He could send Giulio to Venice with letters and full instructions. Giulio, he knew, might be trusted to any extent. So he called the shepherd, wrote a few words on his tablets, and asked him to take them to the osteria.

In a shorter time than he had thought possible, Giulio was at the door of the capanno. Theodore briefly explained his dilemma, announcing in a business-like tone, without note or comment, that there lay Count Raymond very sick and weak, and that he was bound to stay and see him through the Campagna fever.

Giulios eyes shone, and his whole face kindled with the joy that filled his heart at this change in Theodore. But he had tact enough to forbear all expressions of surprise or gratification, merely saying, "Write your pleasure to Venice, Signor Doctor. You can send it by il signor your brother; for of course I stay here with you."

Theodore remonstrated; but Giulio with a purpose was a man of iron, and Theodore had to yield in the end. He resolved to write fully to his father, explaining Gaetanos errors, and entreating him to forgive them, as a personal favour. He had an inward confidence that the boon thus asked would not be denied; for he knew his fathers strong affection for himself and his tenderness towards his eldest son. The only practical difficulty was that of persuading Gaetano to return to Venice without him; and to effect this purpose he found it necessary to go back to the osteria, leaving Giulio in temporary charge of his patient.

So hard was it to accomplish his object, and so many arguments had he to use with Gaetano, that his own resolution was manifestly strengthened by the exercise. But at last he returned to the capanno. " Quick, Giulio!" he said, " come and help me. Another night here were death for him and a terrible risk for us. The miasma rises from the ground when the sun has set, and creeps damp and chill around the sleeper. You and I and the shepherd must take yonder poles, and lash them together with thongs of sheepskin into a kind of rude litter, so as to bring him to the osteria; itself a vile, fever-haunted hole, but at least better than this."

"If he should get a chill?"

"He may die. Left here he must die–that is all. We shall cover him well with sheepskins."

Theodore and Giulio worked energetically, the shepherd assisting them in a nerveless, spiritless way, and yet willingly, so far as his strength went. The move was accomplished just before the sun went down, to Theodores great satisfaction.

Raymond was very ill, and Theodore saw that his symptoms were of the gravest. The fever, itself of an unusually malignant type, found him in a state of mental and bodily exhaustion, which rendered the case almost desperate. As he watched by him through the long hours of the night–for he esteemed his state too critical to leave him in the kind and careful, but unprofessional hands of Giulio–a change stole imperceptibly over his own mind. Raymond was no longer either his friend or his enemy, he was only his " case," his " patient." There awoke within him the strong passion of the physician, the enthusiasm of the knight of science, who fights to save life, and not to destroy it. And never did knight of mediaeval chivalry taste–

"The stern joy which warriors feel
In foemen worthy of their steel,"

more truly than did Theodore when he braced all his powers of mind and body for mortal conflict with his unseen but terrible foe, the fever demon of the Campagna.

Had the malaria in that district been as deadly then as it is now, it is prohable that Theodore would have brought his patient, at any risk, to the nearest village on the hills. But all the evidence we have on the subject goes to show that it has become sensibly worse of late years.

It is true that in ordinary cases it would have been the practice of that age–an age to which Peruvian bark and the country it comes from were alike unknown–to leave the conflict very much to what was called the " vis medicatrix" of Nature, and the malady almost to its own cure. But to Eaymond this course would have been fatal. His was no ordinary case; there were complications which required special and skilful treatment; and the most incessant care and watchfulness were needed so to sustain his failing strength as to give his constitution even the chance of a rally.

For a brief interval Theodore enjoyed that kind of negative truce from inward conflict which results from an intense straining of the faculties towards some object outside of self. The first time he thought it safe to sleep for a few hours, leaving Griulio to take his place, he dreamed that Viola was praising him in her sweet, low voice, for his share in Eaymonds escape from the dungeon. When he awoke his eyes were dim with unaccustomed tears. But the dream helped him; all through the following day Violas face seemed to beam on him, bright with encouragement and approval.

Something else helped him far more efficiently and permanently. Once more the God of his fathers had become for him a real and living Presence. In the darkness of his soul he had cried to God, and God had answered him; therefore God was there. It was the reasoning of a child, yet it might have been also that of a philosopher.

Theodore, all his life, had chosen facts as the sustenance of his soul, refusing to believe anything that did not strike its roots down firmly into the soil of the actual and the real. But his table was made a snare to him, and the things that should have been for his health were to him an occasion of falling. For in worshipping fact he scorned and neglected truth. What the eye cannot see, the ear cannot hear, the finger cannot touch, eluded his analysis. He denied it his faith and his homage; and by that denial he turned his back upon all that is in very deed most real. Thenceforward, the more earnest his search after reality, the farther did he wander away from it, amidst ever-deepening shadows, towards " a land of darkness, as darkness itself."

But that simple, familiar thing–a household word with every child and every peasant–" the difference between right and wrong," could neither be seen, nor heard, nor touched. Yet was it so real that it stood like a wall of adamant between him and his dearest wishes. Not to the eye of sense alone, but also to the eye of intellect there was nothing there; yet, when he tried to cross that invisible, impalpable barrier, he was flung back, as if with the blow of a giant–flung on his face, " with his hand on his mouth and his mouth in the dust." Why should he " let I dare not wait upon I would "? Why could he not dare to do the thing that pleased him, and for which there was no man upon earth to call him to account?

Because, so doing, he would " sin against his own soul," in the strong, true words of his people. What was his soul that he should so regard it, should place its well-being above happiness? It was himself. He knew that righteousness was rather to be chosen than happiness, though he knew not why. He also knew that he was weak: he might choose wrongly, and destroy himself. The cry to "apower outside of ourselves that makes for righteousness " was the irrepressible instinct of his soul, as of all the troubled, the struggling, the suffering, from the beginning to the end of time. But unless this vague "Power" be a "Person," who hears, who cares, who helps, the cries are wasted breath, and the instinct–what Natures instincts never are–implanted but to deceive and betray.

Thus, in the wayside osteria, Theodore came back from the arid creed of Averroes to the better faith of the progenitor of Averroes, the poor Egyptian slave fainting in the desert–" Thou God seest me."

CHAPTER XIX.

COALS OP FIRE.

"I have given
All the gifts required of me–
Hope that blessed me, bliss that crowned,
Love that left me with a wound."

laYMONDS mind wandered at intervals amidst old scenes and vague new bewildering fancies; although, after the first few hours, he recognized Theodore and Giulio, and called them by their names. But he manifested no surprise at being cared for tenderly by Theodore; he seemed to have lost all recollection of their quarrel, and to have gone back to his deliverance from the prison. He evidently confused his transit from the Castle of St. Angelo to the church with the more recent move from the capanno to the osteria, and often he was heard to murmur, "The living took the place of the dead, the dead took the place of the living." He talked of his mother; and of Viola, showing plainly by what he said that their last interview had been of a satisfactory nature; and he repeated, so frequently that Theodore came to know them by heart, the words which had taken such hold upon his memory, "In my Fathers house there are many mansions." Giulio, in his watches by his side, read aloud to him, more than once, the whole of the Gospel from which they are taken, translating it roughly into Italian for his benefit. The monotonous sound seemed to soothe him; but how much, or how little, reached his understanding, was not apparent at the time.

But at last Theodore announced to Giulio with undisguised satisfaction, "I think we shall bring him round. But I have never had a more interesting case, or a more dim cult one."

That evening Baymond looked up, as Theodore stooped over him to administer a cordial. " Theodore, have you forgiven me? " he asked.

"Is not my presence here proof enough of it? " Theodore answered. But he added inwardly, " If thine enemy hunger, feed him; if he thirst, give him drink, saith the law of Jehovah." Going into the outer room, he said to Giulio, "He is decidedly better to-night. I think I may ride to the city to-morrow and get some things that are needed." (Giulio had already done so once or twice.) "You know what to do in my absence."

Giulio readily agreed; and thus he had a long, solitary day with Raymond, who, weak as he still was, undoubtedly felt relieved by the temporary absence of Theodore,

"Giulio," he said, "there is something I want you to do for me when next you visit the city. Think you–could you venture with safety to the Masters house on the Bsquiline?"

"Undoubtedly, Count Raymond."

"The few possessions I left there have of course been taken away during my imprisonment. Indeed, most of the books and clothes were sent to me from time to time, and are doubtless lost for ever now. There was nothing else of value. Except–

what neither friend nor foe would think worth removing–a figure, in clay, not finished. You will find it in the room where I used to sleep. I left it carefully covered with a cloth of blue and crimson tapestry; but that, being rather costly, may have been taken away."

"Well, sir, if I find it?"

"Break it into a thousand pieces, if yoa love me."

"What! Your own work?"

"My own failure. All unworthy of her whom it pretended to represent. Still, I would not have it touched by rude, unloving hands." Then after a pause, and with some impetuosity, "My life seems a failure too. Best it were shattered to fragments, like my work, as indeed I thought it would be–until now."

"Nay, Count Eaymond; that must the Maker decide, not the work."

"I am in a cruel strait. I have unwillingly, yet most really, proved a traitor to Theodore, that best and truest of friends. And he, knowing this, has crushed me altogether by saving my life a second time at the risk of his own."

"You are no traitor, Count Eaymond. You should not call yourself that which you are not. The just man is just to himself as well as to his neighbour."

"Nay, but I am. I hold the signorinas promise. I"

"Signor, do not trouble yourself to explain. It would only agitate you. I perfectly understand the situation. You are the doctors successful rival."

Eaymond bowed his head. " I some times wish I could die, and leave the field clear for him," he said. " Only death could do it–only death."

"Count Raymond, you talk as if your life were your own, to give or to keep. Many a man is very generous with the property of others. Your life belongs first to God; next, to the noble lady to whom you vowed all that man can vow to woman; after that, to your mother, your friends, your fellow-citizens, and your fellow-men."

Raymond was silent and pondered. Giulio resumed after a pause, "My good friend and master, Dr. Theodore, is passing through the waters of a deep and bitter sorrow. You have been the occasion of it, but not the cause. You cannot help him now;–no, not even by your death. The Signorina Viola di Porcaro is not one who would listen to the voice of a new lover with the first scarcely cold in his grave. You would but consign her to the dreary living death of a convent." (Giulio spoke and felt far too bitterly of institutions which after all were the only refuges for unprotected womanhood in those rough and lawless times.) " But there is One who can help him–: the God of his fathers; and I think that even now he is seeking Him who never said to the House of Israel, Seek ye my face in vain."

"You are mistaken there, Giulio. Theodore does not believe in God. He is a Rationalist–a disciple of Averroes."

"He was. But it is not so easy to escape from God. Dr. Theodore may say, as did one of his forefathers, Though I take the wings of the morning, and dwell in the uttermost parts of the sea, even there shall Thy hand lead me, and Thy right hand shau hold me."

"The wings of the morning–the golden rays of the rising sun? I think those were what we were taking–ay, and using them to flee from God."

"How so, Count Raymond?"

"It was all morning with us students. We were as men newly awakened out of a long, deep sleep, and we thought the world around us was awakening too. Our hands had found the priceless stores of ancient learning, art, civilization, and our souls rejoiced over them as over great spoil. We would make them the heritage of all mankind; we would bring back the good old times, which would be indeed the good new times that the whole earth was waiting for. We hoped a worlds redemption from Greek MSS. and Roman antiquities. Ah, Giulio, it was a beautiful dream," he ended, with a sigh.

"The morning light is always beautiful," Giulio said.

"But we floated on its beams away from God. We did not want Him in our new world."

"He wanted you, Count Raymond."

"Ay, He followed us. We felt His hand in the gloomy dungeon–a terrible hand."

"When it strikes. But that is its, and His, strange work. Not when it leads. It is written, Thy hand shall lead me, and. Thy right hand shall hold me. He is leading you now. Eesist Him not."

"Leading me? Ah, whither?"

"Here, to the rest which is the portion of all who trust Him. Hereafter to the many mansions prepared for them."

"If I were quite pure and innocent I might trust God entirely. But do you make no account of our sins?"

"God forbid. Count Raymond, it is with the faithful Christian as it was with you when you escaped from the Castle of St. Angelo. As you often said in your fevered wanderings, The living took the place of the dead, the dead took the place of the living. Christ our Passover was sacrificed for us; He took our place and died for us, then were we accounted dead with Him, so that the law has loosed for ever its claim upon us, and we stand now in His place, acquitted and delivered. Do you understand?"

"I think so: but the words you read in your book are simpler and sweeter. God so loved the world that He gave His only begotten Son. That is a wonderful book, Giulio. It has made the Lord Christ real to me. God of God, Light of Light, very God of very God begotten, as saith the glorious creed my forefathers held so dear, and yet man to the very core and centre of mans wondrous being. Man, not alone hungering, thirsting, wearying–but hoping, fearing, trusting, loving, as you and I do to-day. It seems no presumption, only the deepest of all joys, to say I love Him, and would follow Him if need were to the worlds end, nay, to the uttermost parts of the sea."

"Follow Him, and He will lead you to the Father."

"And to the many mansions.–Giulio, what do those words mean, If it were not so I would have told you?"

"That He is truth, Count Raymond. He keeps no promise to the ear to break it to the heart. He hides nothing; He lets us know the dark as well as the light

Hark! dont you hear horse-hoofs? Here comes Dr. Theodore."

Theodore wore an inscrutable face, and was very silent as to his adventures in the city, but he brought strengthening food and wine, and in his quiet, reserved way, watched Raymond carefully for the next few days. They were days of steady and rapid improvement. He avoided conversation, and left him in great measure to the society of Giulio, who read much to him. Sometimes Theodore came in during the reading, and requested Giulio to go on. On one of these occasions it happened that he heard the concluding chapter of the Gospel of St. John. He said, when the reading was finished, "That is a fine episode in the life of Jesus of Nazareth. It was Simon Peter who denied Him."

"He whom they call the prince of the Apostles, and whose pretended successors claim infallibility," said Giulio; and this time he spoke unadvisedly, for he crossed the current of Theodores not unprofitable thoughts with another thought, which had no special meaning or message for him.

"Yes," answered Theodore, "you Christians have distorted the whole story so hopelessly with your mythological legends, that Jesus and Peter look like monstrous unreal shapes looming through a mist, instead of living human beings. That story is quite human, however. If indeed His nature was not more than human for sweetness and for nobleness, who, cut to the heart by the base treachery of a friend, could not only fling him a scornful I forgive you, but win from his lips that threefold profession of love, charge him to do for Him the work that lay nearest to His heart, and assure him he should one day conquer the very temptation that had conquered him, and die for the Lord he had denied. It is not thus that men forgive each other nowadays."

Raymond knew what was passing in the soul of his friend, and his heart yearned towards him. He stretched out his hand to him with a pleading look.

But Theodore shook his head. " Not yet," he answered coldly but sadly. "I cannot change my own heart, Raymond; but I will do for you all that becomes a man. Listen. You are now convalescent, and there is little danger of a relapse; so I venture to tell you tidings which I have been keeping back since my return from the city the other day. I am not like the false mother who said to King Solomon of the living child, Let it be neither hers nor mine, but rather slay it. I went to the Palazzo Por-caro, and I found that the Signorinas kindred are redoubling their efforts to drive her into a convent. They imagine the Pope has taken umbrage at her presence there, and recent events have made them terribly afraid of his Holiness. You must go in person and solve the difficulty ere it be too late. They will be glad enough to give her to you, as the easiest way out of all their perplexities. But there is no time to be lost."

"Oh, most generous of friends! how can I thank you? But"–the colour faded from his cheek–"how dare I invite her to share my friendless poverty?"

"The Greek professor at Montpellier is dead. You are very young, but your reputation is brilliant, and your misfortunes will not lessen it. I make no doubt you can have his place for the asking, and I will give you a letter which will secure it. I tell you all this not for your sake, but first because it is right, and then because it seems the only chance of happiness left to the Signorina Viola; and whatever I may have suffered I hope I am not coward enough to revenge myself upon her. Go to Rome to-morrow–you are able to travel now, and will be better out of this place–I will lend you any money that may be necessary, but for other help you must depend upon your own resources. The Porcari, as I have said, will make little opposition, or none, and the priest you wot of will do all you need quietly in the church of Santa Maria in Trastevere. A ship in which my father has a venture will leave Ostia in a few days for Marseilles. If you need any further directions, you are not the man I think you. As for me, I am going to Venice, because I long after my fathers house. Giulio, I desire your help and companionship. Pack up what we have here, and follow me to-morrow; I make the first stage of my journey alone this afternoon."

"I will do all you have said; and I wish I had the power to utter the thanks I owe you," said Eaymond, greatly moved.

An hour afterwards Theodore was in the saddle. Raymond came out and once more entreated with touching earnestness that he would give him his hand in token of complete reconciliation.

Theodore extended it, saying, "I give it as a pledge that I have acted towards thee in truth and uprightness. I have done for thee all that man can do for man. And so farewell. God prosper thee."

CHAPTER XX.

VENICE AGAIN.

"Together we have said one prayer,
And sung one vesper strain;
My soul is dim with clouds of care,
Tell me those words again."

JEW things could be more enjoyable than a journey through the plains of beautiful Italia, when the summer heats were over, and the vineyards were laden with their rich clusters of purple and amber, or yielding up their treasures to laughing youths and maidens, whose pleasant labour was almost a holiday. Such a journey was that of Theodore and Giulio, and they made it with every advan tage that money could procure. They slept at the best inns, where, in those days of intellectual activity, the most distinguished literary society was often to be met; and they could command the services of an adequate guard, whenever they had to pass through a district infested with banditti, although, being both of them active and courageous men, they usually preferred relying upon their own resources.

They spent one night at the ancestral home of Campano, and Giulio gave the sorrowing parents a letter with which Raymond had furnished him, containing their sons last message, and other details of mournful interest. These brought comfort; and warm was the gratitude evinced towards the Jewish physician whose kindness had softened the lot of all the captives in the Castle of St. Angelo, though it had been principally intended for Raymond.

The journey ought to have been a holiday pastime, but to one of the two it was a long agony. Theodore ever afterwards remem bered those smiling fields and vineyards as a man might remember the walls of a torture chamber. For his whole life, inward and outward, was being torn up by the roots–roots which were strong and vigorous, which had struck deep and stretched far and wide. The wrench was terrible. The only woman he had ever loved was lost to him irrevocably; and this in itself was a sorrow great enough to fill the mans great heart with anguish. But in losing Viola he lost also his prospect of a settled home, a domestic hearth. All those softening, ennobling, hallowing influences which gather round the idea of the family were for him (as he thought then), never more to exist; no wife was to console him in trouble or sickness; no son was to continue his name amongst men.

Even Work–that silent, modest, unobtrusive comforter, who professes and promises nothing, and yet insensibly wins the mourner from his tears, the sufferer from his pain–seemed about to fail him. How could he go back to Montpellier and tell the band of earnest, intelligent youths, to whom he had been teaching Atheistic Materialism, that he had wholly misread the enigma of the universe? He believed now in Jehovah, and in the first sentence of the Hebrew Scriptures, "In the beginning God created the Heavens and the Earth." What was more, he believed in Jehovah as the God of Righteousness, and in the supreme obligation laid upon himself to be righteous too.

Well, then, had he not acted the part of a righteous man? Had he not, in obedience to the imperative " ought," saved Raymond and given up Viola? He dealt out a stern approval to himself as if he had been another man, but he did not take any pleasure in the contemplation of his own righteousness. He thought of the words of Solomon, "A good man is satisfied from himself," and he tried to realise their truth. But he found self-satisfaction a poor, flavourless, innutritive kind of food, somewhat of the nature of the apples of Sodom.

To Giulio he was impenetrable and unapproachable. That true friend and " camarade " saw the anguish of his soul, and longed to comfort him, with the longing of one who believed that he possessed an infallible panacea for all the sorrows of humanity. " Dr. Theodore is a good man," thought Giulio. " He is true, just, and brave; but he knows, as yet, only the law of Moses, not the gospel of Christ. He has learned, If thine enemy hunger, feed him; but he has not yet learned, Love your enemies. He cannot understand the law of love until his eyes are opened to the love of God that passeth knowledge–that means, to Christ. But he does whatever he knows; and therefore, no doubt, that which he knows not yet God will teach him."

At least he seemed determined to have no other teacher. When he talked to Giulio, and he did so often, it was about the features of the country through which they were journeying, its trees, plants, and flowers; or yet oftener, about " travel in far lands." In the unsettling of all his ties and associations, the passion of his childhood for exploration and discovery seemed to be returning. Many a long hours ride did he beguile for Giulio with tales of the Isles of St. Brandon, and other fair and fleeting dreams that shadowed forth truths yet unknown; or with mysterious passages from the great Arabian philosophers–and especially from Averroes–hinting at undiscovered worlds beyond the Western Sea; or with stories, scarcely less romantic, of the voyages of Marco Polo and the great Portuguese adventurers. He told also of the recent voyages of Christopher Columbus to the Azores and to Iceland, and to these Giulio listened with especial interest, as he himself was by birth a Genoese, and therefore a townsman of Columbus, thotigh his family had removed to Venice in his early childhood.

But always, when they halted for the night, Theodore borrowed Giulios MSS.,, and devoted every spare moment to their perusal. His long residence in the South of France enabled him to master the dialect as easily as Giulio himself. He was especially fascinated by the Gospel of St. John; accounting for the fascination to himself by reflecting that it was the work of a mystic, probably an Alexandrian Platonist, and that mysticism was the natural recoil from the materialism he had been forced to abandon. He considered Giulio a mystic also, though of a peculiar kind; but he did not at all intend to become one himself.

So Venice was reached at last. Theodore brought Giulio to his fathers house, and introduced him there as an honoured guest, to whom he was under many obligations. But, taking him aside as soon as the first social meal was over, he said, "Do me one more kindness, friend Giulio. The Lady Erminia Chalcondyles ought to know her sons safety at once, and to receive his letter. But I have no fancy for a scene, and a ladys tears and thanks, and so forth. You can give her every information she desires just as well as I. Go, my dear fellow, be the bearer of good tidings, and my substitute in a task from which I shrink."

Giulio acquiesced, and took a gondola for the island of Murano. As the rowers shot across the Lagoon, he sat in the little cabin buried in profoundest thought. But when they neared the quay he drew aside the curtain and gazed, as one who sought to drink in every feature of the scene, now bathed in the fair and mellow light of an autumn afternoon. " The place thereof knoweth it no more," he murmured. "Ay, the grass withereth, the flower fadeth, but the word of our God shall stand for ever. Days of youth, how long ago they seem!–Sciar, gondolier, sciar!"

The gondola was touching the steps of the dwelling with which the descriptions of Eaymond had made him so familiar. He sprang up them with a vigour which seemed to show the days of youth not so very far removed, and entered, unchallenged, by the open door. Still he met no one; and, after standing a moment undecided, he saw an inner door ajar, and pushed it open also.

It admitted him into the studio of an artist. This, happily, was not unoccupied. The owner stood with his back to the door and his face to the window, carefully examining a small painting upon glass which he held in his hand. Hearing, however, the steps of an intruder, Giacomo turned, and with a dreamy look and absent manner–for that momentous question whether the colouring of those grapes was quite natural still occupied his mind–inquired the strangers business.

"Scusi, signor. Does the Lady Erminia Chalcondyles live here?"

"Yes, signor; but she has gone forth, with her servant, to hear a sermon in the church yonder." Then, thinking himself scarcely courteous, and attracted besides by an undefined something in the strangers look and manner, he added, "They will return in an hour or so. You are welcome to wait for them here if you please, signor."

Giacomo courteously offered a seat, but Giulio did not take it. The two men stood together, looking each in the others face. Both were advanced in years, though Giulio, really the younger by nearly ten years, looked fully as old as the painter, for the life of the imagination keeps men looking and feeling young. Still, both were grey-haired and travail-worn, as though the storms of the world had beaten upon them. But the expression of Giacomo was gentle, dreamy, sorrowful, unsatisfied; that of Giulio strong, firm, assured, courageous. Yet with all this difference there was a certain likeness, indescribable but real, such as a third person, looking on the two, would have noticed immediately.

Giacomo was the first to speak.

"Signor, favour me, I pray you, with your name. For surely I remember your face. It awakens old associations. No, I cannot be mistaken. I have known you, have I not, in other days?" The words were spoken falteringly, interspersed with breaks and pauses.

"Are yougiacomo Salvi–ormorgagna?" Giulio asked in his turn, for Giacomo was far less changed in every way than himself. " If so, I am your brother–Giovanni Giulio Morgagna."

"Brother?–Gian?–Thank God, He has heard my prayer at last!"

The brothers threw themselves into each others arms, and exchanged a loving brotherly embrace and salutation; a manifestation of feeling sanctioned by the customs of their time and their country.

Giulios life had been a series of adventures, whilst Giacomos had glided tranquilly onwards in the same city, and his faculties found their natural and harmonious development in the direction promised by his childhood. Giulio therefore had the most to tell, Giacamo the most to hear. Before the strange story of the wandering sectary was half ended, the returning footsteps of the Lady Erminia and of Manuel were heard in the passage.

Giacomo led them at once into the studio, found a seat for the lady, and respectfully presented his brother, "Gian Giulio Mor-gagna, who had come to her Excellency with tidings of the young Count."

The sad stillness of a womans life, keeping for long years the same narrow unchanging groove, is often amongst its greatest trials. Through how many vicissitudes had Raymond passed–how much had he learned, felt, suffered, and enjoyed–whilst the current of his mothers life, naturally as intense and strong as that of his own, flowed on noiselessly through a desolate land, without an event to mark its progress. To agonize for him, to weep for him, to pray for him, had been all the work her hand found to do. Had she been a little richer she might have helped other exiles from her native land; had she been a little poorer, the very struggle for subsistence would itself have given her occupation and interest. As it was, the years came and went, finding and leaving her with folded hands, " eating her own heart." No wonder her cheek was blanched, and the ashes which the slaughter of her kindred had sprinkled on her head were changing quickly into snow. Yet it may be that the pain of those sad years was worth the cost–if indeed it had taught her to pray.

Giulio told her of Raymonds sickness and recovery, and of Dr. Theodores care of him; adding that by his advice he was now going to Montpellier, where there was a professorship vacant, which would afford him for the present an honourable occupation and a comfortable asylum. For further particulars he referred her Excellency to the Counts own letter, which he had the honour of placing in her hand. He kept silence upon the subject of Raymonds marriage, not knowing how she might be affected by it; and upon that of his rivalry with Theodore, since, much as he longed to do justice to the magnanimity of his patron, it seemed to him that Raymond alone had the right to tell that story.

Still, he told enough to transport Manuel to the seventh heaven of grateful delight, and to make him bless Dr. Theodore, and Giulio also, by all the Saints in the Greek Calendar. It certainly jarred a little upon his idea of the pretensions of Count Raymond Chalcondyles to imagine him earning his daily bread by teaching the tongue of his forefathers to a crowd of noisy lads in a lecture hall; still he knew that other Greek exiles, as well-born as Raymond, had been thankful to do the same, and, moreover, he had not dwelt so long beneath the roof of Pomponius Laetus, without acquiring some respect for the hierophants of literature. And, after all, what mattered aught else if his young master himself were safe and well?

The Lady Erminia thanked Giulio in fewer words, but with yet deeper feeling. "Tell Dr. Theodore Benedetto," she added, "that the blessing of a widow never yet harmed any man, nor was it ever earned more nobly, or bestowed more heartily, than mine is this day. But, if he permit me, I shall tell him so myself to-morrow."

Having said this, she withdrew to her own apartment, and to the undisturbed enjoyment of Raymonds letter, which had been written in the osteria, in the interval between the departure of Theodore and that of Giulio.

He wrote hopefully about the future; and frankly about his own prospects with regard to Viola, and his relations with Theodore. It was somewhat startling to Erminia to learn that her son, whom she had last seen a boy of fifteen, had by this time actually given her a daughter; but she repressed a rising sigh, and told herself that hers was the common lot of mothers. And her heart was softened by the earnest pleading that followed, that she would come to Montpellier and take up her abode with him. She could make the journey with ease, Raymond said, under the escort of Manuel. Messer Benedetto would secure her a passage in a comfortable ship, and Giulio also would probably be soon returning to what he now accounted his home. " Come to me, dearest mother," he concluded. "My heart yearns to see thy face again; and to repay thee, if I may, for the lonely years thou hast spent for me." The Lady Erminias eyes were wet with happy tears when she folded up the letter.

Meanwhile the stream of talk was flowing rapidly between the long-separated brothers, Giacomo the painter, and Giulio, Gian, or Zun, as he was familiarly called in the Venetian idiom. Each at once took the other to his heart. Their very differences made them dovetail the better (so to speak) into the needs of each others lives. The younger supplied the masculine element–daring, enterprise, boldness–while the nature of the elder, although gentler and more dependent, had a quiet strength of its own, touched into beauty by the rare peculiar grace of artistic genius.

It was a terrible shock to the painter to find that his brother no longer owned allegiance to the Church; the only Church (in Western Christendom) Giacomo had ever heard or dreamed of, whose shrines and altars he spent his days in trying to decorate, and whose observances were linked with every action of his life and every aspiration of his soul.

But Giulio reassured his brother and vindicated himself by a confession of faith that came from depths " below the tide of war"–those regions of the mind that controversy agitates–and was " based on the crystalline sea" of all that is most real in the soul of man. To him, he said, Christ was all in all. He was the Way, the Truth, and the Life. By Him alone we come to the Father. Everything that man has put between his soul and Christ must therefore be swept aside; ay, though it were dear and beautiful as the face of the Madonna, or venerable and awe-inspiring as the chanted psalm or the lifted Host. "The Church has been making one great and terrible mistake, which has involved a thousand more," he added. " She has forgotten the tenderness of Christ. She has ignored His true humanity. She has set before the eyes of mankind the terrors of the law, the powers of the world to come, the awfulness of the great Judge of quick and dead, until, in the Judge, the whole world has forgotten the Saviour. She has taken away the ladder He set up between Heaven and Earth–the ladder which is Himself, the Son of Man–and she has built another of her own contrivance, of which the steps are sacraments, and penances, and saints, and angels, with the blessed Madonna standing at the top. Ah, Giacomo, if men but knew Him as He is–but saw His face!"

"Ah, Zun, my brother, if I could see that face! " sighed Giacomo, with the un satisfied longing of years at his heart. Then, rising from his place, he drew back the cloth that covered his unfinished picture and showed it to Giulio. It was still as far from completion as on the day when Raymond had seen it last.

CHAPTER XXI.

ONE YEAR AFTERWARDS.

JT was, speaking accurately, a year and a half since Raymond, Theodore, and Giulio parted in the little osteria on the Campagna; then the earth was thrilling under the last heats of the summer sun; now the fair Provencal hills and valleys are budding once more into life beneath the first kisses of the spring. But to Raymond the interval seemed brief, partly because it was filled with earnest work, still more because he was happy.

The University of Montpellier had now greatly declined from the high position it occupied during the earlier Middle Ages, principally as a school of medicine. But Theodores great abilities as a teacher, both of medicine and philosophy, perhaps also his bold speculations, which were flavoured with that slight suspicion of heresy daring spirits find rather attractive than otherwise, had given it a strong though temporary impulse. Those who profited largely by this impulse, both in purse and reputation, were eager to welcome the brilliant young Greek, who might do for the Humanities what his friend was doing for the Sciences. " Now," said the heads of the university, " we too shall have our Greek from Constantinople, as good as Chrysolaurns, or Argyropoulos, or Lascaris, or any other distinguished ornament of learning." Nor was Raymonds value, as an attraction to the lecture halls of Montpellier, lessened by his noble birth, or by the persecutions he had endured on account of his attachment to literature, while it was greatly increased by his ability to reproduce the teaching of Pomponius, and to lecture upon the Latin classics with as much facility as upon those of his forefathers. Moreover, he was young, handsome, genial, unassuming. Altogether the university had secured a prize, and was happily conscious of the fact; while as yet there was not time for the smouldering envy of jealous colleagues to break out.

Meanwhile youth and love and hope were transforming a gloomy but substantial dwelling-house in the quaint old city into a genuine home, where all sweet domestic ties and affections might take root and grow. Viola was its presiding spirit; the sunshine of prosperity had ripened her into as near an approach as could readily be found to the poets ideal of the–

"Perfect woman, nobly planned,
To guide, to counsel, to command."

At least there was one, besides Raymond, who considered her perfect. That was Eaymonds mother. Could more be said for the young wife?

Lately a new inmate had come to that home–" out of the everywhere into the here," a precious gift of God, and at once, an object, of deepest love and a source of pride to the whole household, but the last especially to the aged Manuel, who thought the birth of a Dauphin of France an event of trifling importance compared with that of an heir to the house of Chalcondyles.

The young professor was now almost as light-hearted as the schoolboy who went singing from the academy of Venice to his home in Murano, and he was far more truly happy. Yet, strange to say, the one sorrow that lay in the depths of the mans heart–veiled indeed with many a flower, but still there–was the very same that in those old days spoiled the artless pleasures of the boy. " Mother," he said, when the name of his firstborn came to be discussed, "let me have my will this time. My fathers shade will forgive me. I must needs call my boy Theodore."

He had his will, all the more easily because Theodore chanced to be a good and much-used Greek name, which had been borne by some of his mothers kindred.

It seemed as though the christening of the child was destined to bring a joy long wished for in vain. A few days after the important event the little family were seated together at their evening meal, when Manuel opened the door and announced, in a tone almost as quiet and ordinary as though it had been merely one of their very frequent student visitors, "Dr. Theodore Benedetto."

The grave, middle-aged physician, for such he looked now, was greeted by all affectionately, by Eaymond with emotion he could scarcely conceal. Theodore had long since by letter resigned his post at the university, so that his appearance was the more unexpected and surprising. His manner was kind, and his look and voice unusually gentle; but now, as ever, he shrank from manifestations of feeling.

In answer to many an eager question, he gave, very quietly and naturally, an account of himself since their parting. " I found iny father out of health and depressed by many cares," he said. "Both as son and as physician I could be of use to him. My brother Gaetano had not been fortunate or prudent, and his affairs caused him much anxiety. But now at last all is happily settled. I brought Gaetano with me to Marseilles and established him there in a good business. As for myself, the roving instinct has come over me again; and Giulio also wished to revisit Languedoc."

"Then he is with you?"

"Yes; I left him at the Inn."

"Can you suppose for a moment that you, or he, are going to stay there? Manuel shall fetch him at once, and shall give directions to have your baggage brought also."

Theodore began to make some opposition, but apparently recollecting himself, yielded. As Viola was about to leave the room " on hospitable cares intent," he detained and inquired for the child of bis friend.

"I will bring him," said Viola.

While she did so, Raymond asked for Giacomo. " He seems to have grown young again since he found a brother in Giulio," Theodore answered. " The two are the closest of friends. He has just completed a picture which is much and deservedly praised in Venice. The best judges say it is equal to anything produced by either of the G-entili brothers. The subject is Christ Healing a Blind Man."

Then the wonder and treasure of the house was exhibited, and Theodore performed the homage expected from him sufficiently, and even gracefully. " Of course he is another Raymond?"

"No," Raymond answered. " We have named him after the dearest friend we have ever had, or shall have, Theodore."

Greatly moved, Theodore turned aside, and no more was said until the child was borne away by Viola, the Lady Erminia following. Even then the words were few.

"Theodore, you have pardoned?"

"What there was to pardon," Theodore answered with a hand-clasp that said more than words. "You, too, had something to forgive."

"Nothing, except benefits."

"Thrown to you as bones to a dog. Kay-mond, if yours had not been the sweetest of natures, you would have hated me bitterly. I was proud then, for I had not learned my own need of pardon. I am wiser now, I hope. At least I know now how far from wise I was, and am."

"Dear Theodore, why not return here, where you are so loved and longed for? Your splendid successes as a teacher are in every ones mouth; and every one marvels at your abandoning prospects such as yours."

"Kaymond, I could no longer expound Averroes. I am changed in many things. What of your buried treasure, my friend?"

"Circumstances have made me a laggard in the very matter you would have expected me to pursue most eagerly. First, I had to establish myself here, to give a home to my wife and mother, and so forth. Then, I had to ascertain particulars about the locality, and to arrange my plans. Just as all that was finished, a new student arrived here, a gay and gallant Provencal, who attracted me at once, and who proved on inquiry to be no other than the present Lord of Vaudelon."

"Why should that hinder you?"

"The boy has attached himself to me; he follows me everywhere like my shadow. In short, he renders me the same kind of homage we used to render in old times to Pomponius Laetus. The incense is sweet, Theodore."

"I too have found it so."

"But embarrassing, in this instance. How, on the one hand, can I say to him, My dear boy, your broad acres belonged to my forefathers, from whom yours have taken them by robbery and violence? How, on the other, can I creep like a thief into his domains, and dig up his garden without asking his leave?"

"We shall see that," said Theodore, changed indeed in many things, as he said, but prompt and resolute as ever.

A few days afterwards Theodore, Eaymond, and Giulio were spurring gaily over the plains of Languedoc, on their way to the hills of St. Peray, where was the Castle of Vaudelon. The young lord of Vaudelon, who was fully aware of their errand and much interested in its results, had warmly recommended them to the hospitality of his mother and sisters.

Thus it happened that Eaymond actually entered the rose garden under the guidance of a fair lady, as in the dream of his childhood; only he always believed that the lady of his dream wore the features of Viola. This lady was the widowed chatelaine, a dignified personage, who, attended by a bower-maiden of gentle blood, sat in the arbour, and watched the proceedings of Raymond and his friends.

The fragment of parchment in Eaymonds reliquary had been carefully studied before hand, and the measurements it contained were now accurately marked off. Then came the anxious moment. Eaymond took the spade first, then Giulio relieved him.

"There is nothing, I am sure," Eaymond said at length with a half sigh. A formidable heap of clay had been thrown up without any result.

"Do not despair yet," interposed Theodore, who was leaning on his cane. " Take care, Giulio; you will break that spade."

"I have struck it against a stone," said Giulio. " No. Wait. I verily believe we have found it!"

What looked like a mass of rotten leaves was soon brought to light and laid upon the grass. Within the leaves were many wrappings of skin, half-decayed; and when these were torn off or cut away, a box appeared, made of some dark-coloured wood and clamped with iron. It was about two feet square and of considerable weight, although, Kaymond thought, scarcely heavy enough to contain gold.

There was no lock, only a kind of rude clasp, which Raymond with much difficulty succeeded in unfastening, while Theodore, Giulio, and the two ladies watched him in silence. At last he drew out a great MS. volume and laid it on the grass. " That is all / " he said, turning to Theodore with a long sigh of disappointment.

He was a brave man, but he could not resign the vague, yet cherished, hope of years without a pang. Better to have left his treasure still in the border land between dream and expectation! "No doubt books were very precious in those benighted days," he said rather bitterly. " Still, I marvel at the words of my ancestor, that lands and castle were well lost for this, and little worth without it."

Giulio meanwhile threw himself on the grass and began carefully to examine the book. Presently he cried out in a kind of rapture, "It is the Bible, the whole Bible! Gods own Word, from Genesis to Kevela-tion! God be praised!"

He was right. The Old Testament was in Latin, in fact it was only a copy of the Vulgate; but the New had been translated into the Provencal of the twelfth century, the Langue doc, the tongue of the Troubadours. Both were complete, and enriched with many notes. " Signor Count," he said to Raymond, " you may be proud of your ancestors. They were amongst Gods hidden suffering people. The law of His mouth was dearer unto them than thousands of gold and silver. For their sakes, no doubt, He hath a favour unto you."

It was to Raymonds honour that, after a thoughtful pause, he stooped and took up the volume, reverently pressing it to his heart. " Since God has sent it to me in so strange a way," he said, "He must have something to teach me through its pages. Pray for me, good and true friends, that what He teaches my soul may be ever open to learn."

CHAPTER XXII.

MANY TBARS AFTERWARDS.

"So take and use Thy work,
Amend what flaws may lurk,

What strain o the stuff, what warpings past the aim.
My times be in Thy hand;
Perfect the cup as planned;
Let age approve of youth, and death complete the same."

HAT segment of a human life which can be severed from its antecedents and its results, and laid bare for inspection by the hand of a chronicler, must needs be only a part, perhaps it is a very subordinate part, of the whole. Life is not over when the vicissitudes of a stormy youth have passed, and the man that these have trained and disciplined sets his face steadily, though it may be silently, to the toils and cares of a busy manhood. If the banquet be of Gods spreading, assuredly the best wine will be kept for the last; the blessings of the sultry noon will abound above the mornings glow and glory; and when in its appointed season noon gives place to evening, and evening again to night, still His law of progress will hold good, and night itself prove the morning of a brighter and better day.

Never yet was home or heart which twenty years passed over and left no trace behind. Long before such an interval as this had glided by, Eaymonds dwelling-place had ceased to be in sunny Languedoc, the land of his boyish dreams. We may visit him once again in the home he has chosen, a German home, amongst men and women who speak a German tongue, and look at him with kind, frank, German eyes, blue as their own sky. It is on the Bohemian side of the romantic mountain range which separates that country from Saxony. There, in a secluded village, a colony of "United Brethren" have found shelter and refuge from persecution amidst "the strength of the hills." Raymond is their pastor, but he is much more besides, he is the preceptor, guide, and counsellor of a chosen band of young men, who have come to him from all parts of the land to be educated for the ministry of the Church of " Reformers before the Reformation."

Is it one of these who stands before him now–a fine athletic, dark-eyed young man, who looks reverently and inquiringly into the pastors thoughtful face? Not so; that is Raymonds eldest son, Theodore Chalcon-dyles, and Theodore will be no pastor, the familiar beaten paths of home not always proving the most attractive to young eager feet. Moreover, another influence has been at work upon him; but it is an influence not antagonistic to his fathers, and his father is content.

"There is no reason why you should not take out your degree at Montpellier," Eaymond is saying to his son. "Whatever you do afterwards will be done the better by you as a duly licensed physician."

"Father," said the young man, "you taught Greek at Montpellier for several years; they remember you there, and with honour. Why did you leave it?"

Eaymond smiled, took a large and heavy volume of MS. from one of his bookshelves and laid it on the table. " That did it," he said.

"You have often told us how you found it, and how precious it is to you, my father. But why should it so change all the circumstances of your life?"

"The New Testament in the old Provencal language sent me back to the study of the original Greek; and to that study I owe the opening out before me of new worlds of thought and knowledge. I had already a dim but real love for the Word of God, and for Him of whom it testifies, thanks to one whose name I have ever taught you to honour."

"Giulio Morgagna. Do you know, father, where he is now?"

"I last heard of him as the instructor of a company of glass-makers in the mountains of Foix. He is likely to teach them much more than the mysteries of their craft. If indeed he escape

"I taught many things out of that book to the students at Montpellier. I sought to make them Grecians, not so much after the manner of Plato as after that of Apollos, or rather of those who expounded unto Apollos the way of the Lord more perfectly. But as I learned more and more of that way myself, many things perplexed and disquieted me. My position was becoming every day more difficult and painful, when God sent me the guidance I was longing for. A deputation from the Evangelical Church of the United Brethren was passing noiselessly up and down through the great evil world of Christendom; searching everywhere, if perchance any might be found who had understanding and sought after God, and whose souls, touched by Divine truth, revolted against a religion of empty forms and ceremonies. To me their scriptural creed, their simple worship, their apostolic life offered just what my soul desired, and therefore I accompanied them when they returned here. To my mother the change was made easy by the connection between the Bohemian Churches and those of the East, whence their Christianity was originally derived. To my aged friend and servant Manuel, already near his departure, it seemed, as he said, like going home to die amongst his own people. For he chose to consider the Calixtines true orthodox believers, and great was his joy when, first with them and afterwards with us, he drank of the Cup to which they have so bravely vindicated the right of all the faithful. To my children too this has been a happy home; although the elder are now pluming their wings for flight, you towards the West, and my young artist Raymond–since he must needs be a sculptor–towards that sweet southern clime where my own boyhood was spent. Still, wherever you roam, the faith learned here will be treasured in your hearts. We are a small, despised, persecuted remnant; yet, Theodore, we are sons of the morning. I think the future of the world is with us, or with such as we are."

The glass-makers of Foix, a very interesting community, were ennobled by Charles VI. They early gave in their adhesion to the principles of the Reformation, to which they continued steadfastly attached, in spite of the most cruel persecutions, until the time of the French Revolution.

A fact. This was the second deputation sent for this purpose by the United Brethren. But " their emissaries found, with the exception of a small number of Waldenses, only a few isolated believers, several of whom perished in the flames before their eyes. The Brethren then waited with resignation until God should come to the succour of His Church and His people."

"And," said Theodore, "with the men of science, who explore nature."

"I deny it not. In the beginning was the Word–all things were made by Him, and without Him was not anything made that was made. Therefore, all created things are Gods utterance, the expression of His thought. Go then, my son, read what He has said in that great book of which the leaves are earth and ocean, and the letters stars and flowers and living things without number. I keep to this " (he laid his hand on the

Bible) " as my work and my joy, and my meditation day and night. I believe that in both there are wondrous things–treasures yet undreamed of–which He is keeping to reward the earnest seeker."

"So says Dr. Theodore. About that world beyond the Western wave, he is more and more assured every day, he and his friend, the great navigator Christopher Columbus."

"Theodore, I trust utterly the man after whom I named you; and whom, from my boyhood upwards, I have loved as a brother. Of the affection he has shown you and the benefits you have received from him we need not speak, both of us know them well. And since, long years ago, I learned from his own lips that his heart acknowledged Jesus of Nazareth as his Messiah and his Saviour, mine has been at rest about him. I have always wished you to regard him in the light of a second father. Therefore, if it be his desire that you should go with him to the ends of the earth, and if it be the desire of your own soul also, God forbid that I should say you nay."

Theodores eyes sparkled. " It is his desire," he said, " and mine. He is now aiding Columbus by every means in his power to bring his projects of discovery before some prince or commonwealth able to translate dreams into deeds. For, as I have said, he believes, with Columbus, that there is beyond the Western Sea a great undiscovered land (connected no doubt with India), and his determination is fixed to go and see it before he dies. Father, it is to that land he would have me go with him."

"Then go, and God prosper thee and him. Go, far as you will, on the wings of the morning; and, whithersoever you go, may His hand lead you, His right hand hold you."

THE END.

I, HWIN BROTHERS, THE GBESEAM PRESS, CHILWORTH AND LONDON.

CPSIA information can be obtained at www.ICGtesting.com
Printed in the USA
244307LV00001B/129/P

9 780217 606561